SOU H

D0822040

EDITED BY ESTHER MENON

A WRITER'S CAULDRON

A NEW WINDMILL COLLECTION
INVESTIGATING GENRES

Heinemann
New Windmills

`Published by Heinemann Educational Publishers
Halley Court, Jordan Hill, Oxford OX2 8EJ
A division of Reed Educational and Professional Publishing Ltd

OXFORD MELBOURNE AUCKLAND
JOHANNESBURG BLANTYRE GABORONE
IBADAN PORTSMOUTH (NH)USA CHICAGO

04 03 02
10 9 8 7 6 5 4 3 2 1

ISBN: 0 435 12545 1

Acknowledgements
The publishers gratefully acknowledge the following for permission to reproduce
copyright material. Every effort has been made to trace copyright holders, but in some
cases has proved impossible. The publishers would be happy to hear from any copyright
holder that has not been acknowledged.

J.S.F. Burrage for 'The Sweeper' by A. M. Burrage, from *Charles Keepings Book of Classic
Ghost Stories* published by Blackie & Sons 1986; Laura Cecil Literary Agency on behalf of
the author's estate for 'The Boys' Toilets' by Robert Westall, from *Ghost Stories Chosen
By Robert Westall* published by Kingfisher 1988. Copyright © Robert Westall 1988;
'Hansel and Gretel' by The Brothers Grimm; The Estate of Angela Carter c/o Rogers,
Coleridge & White Limited, 20 Powis Mews, London W11 1JN for 'The Werewolf' by
Angela Carter. Copyright © Angela Carter 1979; 'The Adventure of the Sussex Vampire'
by Sir Arthur Conan Doyle; Oxford University Press for 'The Knight's Tale' by Geoffrey
Chaucer retold by Geraldine McCaughrean, from *The Canterbury Tales* published by
Oxford University Press; John Johnson Limited for 'Cinderella Girl' by Vivien Alcock.
Copyright © Vivien Alcock; David Higham Associates Limited for 'Lamb to the Slaughter'
by Roald Dahl, from *Someone Like You* published by Penguin Books; David Higham
Associates Limited for 'Gift' by Susan Gates. Copyright © Susan Gates 1998; Don
Congdon Associates Inc, New York for 'A Sound of Thunder' by Ray Bradbury. Copyright
© 1952 Crowell Collier Publishing Company. Renewed 1980 by Ray Bradbury; Writers
House, New York for 'Mind Bend' by Martin Martinsen, first published in *Spacers:
A collection of science fiction stories* chosen by R. Davis published by Hutchinson Junior
Books in 1979; 'The Tomb of Sarah' by F. G. Loring, first published in Pall Mall Magazine
December 1990; Time Warner Books UK for extract from *Interview With A Vampire* by
Anne Rice published by Time Warner Books in the UK by arrangement with
Alfred A. Knopf Inc. Copyright © 1976 Anne O'Brien Rice.

Cover by Jo Parry
Cover design by The Point
Illustrations: The Sweeper – Neil Parker, The Adventure of the Sussex Vampire –
Mark Oldroyd, The Sweet Shop and The Knights Tale – David Hopkins,
A Sound of Thunder – Hashim Akib, The Tomb of Sarah – John Holder
Typeset by ↗ Tek-Art, Croydon, Surrey
Printed and bound in the United Kingdom by Clays Ltd, St Ives plc

Tel: 01865 888058 www.heinemann.co.uk

Contents

Horror stories

For Sam

Introduction for students

When I was asked by the publisher what I would like to call this book about 'genres' of literature, I decided not to use the word 'genre' in the main title. I know from asking that many people are not familiar with the word and if I used it in the title how would it then encourage lots of readers to pick this up from the shelf?

The main focus of this book is to include a variety of good stories that students of your age would really enjoy. As the front cover suggests, there are many ingredients available to writers of stories. One of the choices open to them is to write with a 'genre' in mind – that is, to write within a given tradition. For example, ghosts, eerie settings and suspense are typical of stories written in the supernatural genre. Happy endings, wicked stepmothers and princesses are the ingredients of the typical fairytale genre.

However, many modern authors have decided to play around with some of these styles. The long history of literature written in recognisable genres has meant that there is a large body of texts that readers and writers know well. Authors can now draw on these traditions to develop them further; and so we have modern versions of fairytales, not written for children, as you will find here in *Sweet Shop* and *The Werewolf*, detective stories where the police, not the murderers, are caught out, and vampire stories where the vampires themselves laugh at the old wives' tales of their fear of garlic and priests.

This book will help you to recognise the common features of traditional genres in your reading, and discover how these conventions offer valid and exciting opportunities for your own writing. I hope you enjoy the variety of ingredients in this writers' cauldron.

Esther Menon

Introduction for teachers

Putting together a collection of stories that 'defines' genre is somewhat contentious. If university academics can write whole theses questioning these terms, who are we to set hard and fast definitions for secondary students of literature in the space of a small hardback? I have not aimed therefore to set concrete criteria for the genre addressed here, but have provided some clear examples of writing that are consciously written within a genre and some that deliberately manipulate the genre. The collection here therefore supports the Year 8 framework objective of recognising the conventions of some common genres of writing.

The balance of pre and post-twentieth century literature will meet the needs of a relatively wide ability range within the Key Stage 3 classroom. I have aimed to order the stories as graduating in difficulty. The love, ghost and fairytale stories offer the most accessible introduction to the study of genre, whereas the language of the vampire stories is more demanding. Most texts are appropriate for individual reading, though teachers may want to address the use of 'bad language' in *The Boys' Toilets* (page 18), be aware of the religious sensitivities of some pupils when using the ghost and vampire stories, and discuss the issues of arranged marriages in *Gift* (page 124).

Each story begins with some background notes for the students and a point to consider as they read through the text. The related activities at the back of the book offer questions to develop reading and understanding. They are followed by reading, writing or speaking and listening activities linked to the text, some encompassing ICT skills. Both questions and activities have been written in the context of the English Framework at Key Stage 3, mostly addressing text level objectives, but including some word and sentence level coverage where appropriate.

For easy reference, a chart beginning on page 240 sets out the Framework objectives met by each story and its activities.

I hope the ingredients here offer you and your classes substantial food for thought!

Esther Menon

Ghost stories

Ghost stories have been popular for many years. In this section, we look at two stories that were written several years apart. Despite that, each contains traditional elements of the genre.

The Sweeper – A M Burrage

Alfred Burrage was born in Middlesex in 1889 and died in 1956. Many of his short stories are of the horror or supernatural genres. Traditional ghost stories often begin with some kind of mystery and a setting that has links with the past. As you read this story and do the activities on page 215, consider how far this story fits with what you might expect in a traditional ghost story.

The Boys' Toilets – Robert Westall

Robert Westall wrote the award-winning novels *The Machine-Gunners, The Scarecrows, Blitzcat* and *The Kingdom By The Sea*. His writing spans many literary genres. Despite the modern setting and language of this eerie story, Westall draws on many of the traditional elements of a ghost story, such as a setting with links to the past and past events that need to be avenged.

The Sweeper
A M Burrage

It seemed to Tessa Winyard that Miss Ludgate's strangest characteristic was her kindness to beggars. This was something more than a little peculiar in a nature which, to be sure, presented a surface like a mountain range of unexpected peaks and valleys; for there was a thin streak of meanness in her. One caught glimpses of it here and there, to be traced a little way and lost, like a thin elusive vein in a block of marble. One week she would pay the household bills without a murmur; the next she would simmer over them in a mild rage, questioning the smallest item, and suggesting the most absurd little economies which she would have been the first to condemn later if Mrs Finch the housekeeper had ever taken her at her word. She was rich enough to be indifferent, but old enough to be crotchety.

Miss Ludgate gave very sparsely to local charities, and those good busybodies who went forth at different times with subscription lists and tales of good causes often visited her and came empty away. She had plausible, transparent excuses for keeping her purse-strings tight. Hospitals should be State-aided; schemes for assisting the local poor destroyed thrift; we had heathen of our own to convert, and needed to send no missionaries abroad. Yet she was sometimes overwhelmingly generous in her spasmodic charities to individuals, and her kindness to itinerant beggars was proverbial among their fraternity. Her neighbours were not grateful to her for this, for it was said that she encouraged every doubtful character who came that way.

When she first agreed to come on a month's trial Tessa Winyard had known that she would find Miss Ludgate difficult, doubting whether she would be able to retain the post of companion, and, still more, if she would want to retain it. The thing was not arranged through the reading and answering of an advertisement. Tessa knew a married niece of the old lady who, while recommending the young girl to her ancient kinswoman, was able to give Tessa hints as to the nature and treatment of the old lady's crotchets. So she came to the house well instructed and not quite as a stranger.

We have her writing home to her 'Darling Mother' as follows:

I expect when I get back home again our dear old rooms will look absurdly small. I thought at first that the house was huge, and every room as big as a barrack-room – not that I've ever been in a barrack-room! But I'm getting used to it now, and really it isn't so enormous as I thought. Huge compared with ours, of course, but not so big as Lord Branbourne's house, or even Colonel Exted's.

Really, though, it's a darling old place and might have come out of one of those books in which there's a Mystery, and a Sliding Panel, and the heroine's a nursery governess who marries the Young Baronet. But there's no mystery that I've heard of, although I like to pretend there is, and even if I were the nursery governess there's no young baronet within a radius of miles. But at least it ought to have a traditional ghost, although, since I haven't heard of one, it's probably deficient even in that respect! I don't like to ask Miss Ludgate, because, although she's a dear, there are questions I couldn't ask her. She might believe in ghosts and it might scare her to talk about them; or she mightn't, and then she'd be furious with me for talking rubbish. Of course, I know it's all rubbish, but it would be very nice to know that we were supposed to be haunted by a nice Grey Lady – of, say about the period of Queen Anne. But if we're haunted by nothing else, we're certainly haunted by tramps.

Her letter went on to describe the numerous daily visits of those nomads of the English countryside, who beg and steal on their way from workhouse to workhouse; those queer, illogical, feckless beings who prefer the most intense miseries and hardships to the comparative comforts attendant on honest work. Three or four was a day's average of such callers, and not one went empty away. Mrs Finch had very definite orders, and she carried them out with the impassive face of a perfect subject of discipline. When there was no spare food there was the pleasanter alternative of money which could be transformed into liquor at the nearest inn.

Tessa was for ever meeting these vagrants in the drive. Male and female, they differed in a hundred ways; some still trying to cling to the last rags of self-respect, others obscene, leering, furtive, potential criminals who lacked the courage to rise above petty theft. Most faces were either evil or carried the rolling eyes and lewd, loose mouth of the semi-idiot, but they were all alike in their personal uncleanliness and in the insolence of their bearing.

Tessa grew used to receiving from them direct and insolent challenges of the eyes, familiar nods, blatant grins. In their several ways they told her that she was nobody and that, if she hated to see them, so much the better. They knew she was an underling, subject to dismissal, whereas they, for some occult reason, were always the welcome guests. Tessa resented their presence and their dumb insolence, and secretly raged against Miss Ludgate for encouraging them. They were the sewer-rats of society, foul, predatory, and carrying disease from village to village and from town to town.

The girl knew something of the struggles of the decent poor. Her upbringing in a country vicarage had given her intimate knowledge of farm-hands and builders' labourers, the tragic poverty of their homes, their independence and their gallant struggles for existence. On Miss Ludgate's estate there was more than one family living on bread and potatoes and getting not too much of either. Yet the old lady had no sympathy for them, and gave unlimited largesse to the undeserving. In the ditches outside the park it was always possible to find a loaf or two of bread flung there by some vagrant who had feasted more delicately on the proceeds of a visit to the tradesmen's door.

It was not for Tessa to speak to Miss Ludgate on the subject. Indeed, she knew that – in the phraseology of the servants' hall – it was as much as her place was worth. But she did mention it to Mrs Finch, whose duty was to provide food and drink, or, failing those, money.

Mrs Finch, taciturn through her environment but still with an undercurrent of warmth, replied at first with the one pregnant word, 'Orders!' After a moment she added: 'The mistress has her own good reasons for doing it – or thinks she has.'

It was late summer when Tessa first took up her abode at Billington Abbots, and sweet lavender, that first herald of the approach of autumn, was already blooming in the gardens. September came and the first warning gleams of yellow showed among the trees. Spiked chestnut husks opened and dropped their polished brown fruit. At evenings the ponds and the trout stream exhaled pale, low-hanging mists. There was a cold snap in the air.

By looking from her windows every morning Tessa marked on the trees the inexorable progress of the year. Day by day the green tints lessened as the yellow increased. Then yellow began to give place to gold and brown and red. Only the hollies and the laurels stood fast against the advancing tide.

There came an evening when Miss Ludgate appeared for the first time in her winter shawl. She seemed depressed and said little during dinner, and afterwards in the drawing-room, when she had taken out and arranged a pack of patience cards preparatory to beginning her evening game, she suddenly leaned her elbows on the table and rested her face between her hands.

'Aren't you well, Miss Ludgate?' Tessa asked anxiously.

She removed her hands and showed her withered old face. Her eyes were piteous, fear-haunted, and full of shadows.

'I am very much as usual, my dear,' she said. 'You must bear with me. My bad time of the year is just approaching. If I can live until the end of November I shall last another year. But I don't know yet – I don't know.'

'Of course you're not going to die this year,' said Tessa, with a robust note of optimism which she had found useful in soothing frightened children.

'If I don't die this autumn it will be the next, or some other autumn,' quavered the old voice. 'It will be in the autumn that I shall die. I know that. I know that.'

'But how can you know?' Tessa asked, with just the right note of gentle incredulity.

'I know it. What does it matter how I know? . . . Have many leaves fallen yet?'

'Hardly any as yet,' said Tessa. 'There has been very little wind.'

'They will fall presently,' said Miss Ludgate. 'Very soon now . . .'

Her voice trailed away, but presently she rallied, picked up the miniature playing cards, and began her game.

Two days later it rained heavily all the morning and throughout the earlier part of the afternoon. Just as the light was beginning to wane, half a gale of wind sprang up, and showers of yellow leaves, circling and eddying at the wind's will, began to find their way to earth through the level slant of the rain. Miss Ludgate sat watching them, her eyes dull with the suffering of despair, until the lights were turned on and the blinds were drawn.

During dinner the wind dropped again and the rain ceased. Tessa afterwards peeped between the blinds to see still silhouettes of trees against the sky, and a few stars sparkling palely. It promised after all to be a fine night.

As before, Miss Ludgate got out her patience cards, and Tessa picked up a book and waited to be bidden to go to the piano. There was silence in the room save for intermittent sounds of cards being laid with a snap upon the polished surface of the table, and occasional dry rustlings as Tessa turned the pages of her book.

. . . When she first heard it Tessa could not truthfully have said. It seemed to her that she had gradually become conscious of the sounds in the garden outside, and when at last they had so forced themselves upon her attention as to set her wondering what caused them it was impossible for her to guess how long they had actually been going on.

Tessa closed the book over her fingers and listened. The sounds were crisp, dry, long-drawn-out, and rhythmic. There was an equal pause after each one. It was rather like listening to the leisurely brushing of a woman's long hair. What was it? An uneven surface being scratched by something crisp and pliant? Then Tessa knew. On the long path behind the house which travelled the whole length of the building somebody was sweeping up the fallen leaves with a stable broom. But what a time to sweep up leaves!

She continued to listen. Now that she had identified the sounds they were quite unmistakable. She would not have had to guess twice had it not been dark outside, and the thought of a gardener showing such devotion to duty as to work at that hour had at first been rejected by her subconscious mind. She looked up, with the intention of making some remark to Miss Ludgate – and she said nothing.

There was a movement in the unnaturally silent room. Miss Ludgate had turned her head, and now showed her companion a white face of woe and doom-ridden eyes. Then, in a flash, her expression changed. Tessa knew that Miss Ludgate had caught her listening to the sounds from the path outside, and that for some reason the old lady was annoyed with her for having heard them. But why? And why that look of terror on the poor, white old face?

'Won't you play something, Tessa?'

Despite the note of interrogation, the words were an abrupt command, and Tessa knew it. She was to drown the noise of sweeping from outside, because, for some queer reason, Miss Ludgate did not want her to hear it. So, tactfully, she played pieces which allowed her to make liberal use of the loud pedal.

After half an hour Miss Ludgate rose, gathered her shawl tighter about her shoulders, and hobbled to the door, pausing on the way to say good night to Tessa.

Tessa lingered in the room alone and reseated herself before the piano. A minute or two elapsed before she began to strum softly and absent-mindedly. Why did Miss Ludgate object to her hearing that sound of sweeping from the path outside? It had ceased now or she would have peeped out to see who actually was at work. Had Miss Ludgate some queer distaste for seeing fallen leaves lying about, and was she ashamed because she was keeping the gardener at work at that hour? But it was unlike Miss Ludgate to mind what people thought of her; besides, she rose late in the morning, and there would be plenty of time to brush away the leaves before the mistress of the house could set eyes on them. And then, why was Miss Ludgate so terrified? Had it anything to do with her queer belief that she would die in the autumn?

On her way to bed Tessa smiled gently to herself for having tried to penetrate to the secret places of a warped mind which was over eighty years old. She had just seen another queer phase of Miss Ludgate, and all of such seemed inexplicable.

The night was still calm and promised so to remain.

'There won't be many more leaves down tonight,' Tessa reflected as she undressed.

But when next morning she sauntered out into the garden before breakfast the long path which skirted the rear of the house was still thickly littered with them, and Toy, the second gardener, was busy among them with a barrow and one of those birch stable brooms which, in medieval imaginations, provided steeds for witches.

'Hullo!' exclaimed Tessa. 'What a lot of leaves must have come down last night!'

Toy ceased sweeping and shook his head.

'No, miss. This 'ere little lot come down with the wind early part o' the evenin'.'

'But surely they were all swept up. I heard somebody at work here after nine o'clock. Wasn't it you?'

The man grinned.

'You catch any of us at work arter nine o'clock, Miss!' he said. 'No, miss, nobody's touched 'em till now. 'Tes thankless work, too. So soon as you've swept up one lot there's another waitin'. Not a hundred men could keep this 'ere garden tidy this time o' the year.'

Tess said nothing more and went thoughtfully into the house. The sweeping was continued off and on all day, for more leaves descended, and a bonfire built up on the waste ground beyond the kitchen garden wafted its fragrance over to the house.

That evening Miss Ludgate had a fire made up in the boudoir and announced to Tessa that they would sit there before and after dinner. But it happened that the chimney smoked, and after coughing and grumbling, and rating Mrs Finch on the dilatoriness and inefficiency of sweeps, the old lady went early to bed.

It was still too early for Tessa to retire. Having been left to herself she remembered a book which she had left in the drawing-room, and with which she purposed sitting over the dining-room fire. Hardly had she taken two steps past the threshold of the drawing-room when she came abruptly to a halt and stood listening. She could not doubt the evidence of her ears. In spite of what Toy had told her, and that it was now after half past nine, somebody was sweeping the path outside.

She tiptoed to the window and peered out between the blinds. Bright moonlight silvered the garden, but she could see nothing. Now, however, that she was near the window, she could locate the sounds more accurately, and they seemed to proceed from a spot farther down the path which was hidden from her by the angle of the window setting. There was a door just outside the room giving access to the garden, but for no reason that she could name she felt strangely unwilling to go out and look at the mysterious worker. With the strangest little cold thrill she was aware of a distinct preference for seeing him – for the first time, at least – from a distance.

Then Tessa remembered a landing window, and after a little hesitation she went silently and on tiptoe upstairs to the first floor, and down a passage on the left of the stairhead. Here moonlight penetrated a window and threw a pale blue screen upon the opposite wall. Tessa fumbled with the window fastenings, raised the sash softly and silently, and leaned out.

On the path below her, but some yards to her left and close to the angle of the house, a man was slowly and rhythmically sweeping with a stable broom. The broom swung and struck the path time after time with a soft, crisp *swish*, and the strokes were as regular as those of the pendulum of some slow old clock.

From her angle of observation she was unable to see most of the characteristics of the figure underneath. It was that of a working man, for there was something in the silhouette subtly suggestive of old and baggy clothes. But apart from all else there was something queer, something odd and unnatural, in the scene on which she gazed. She knew that there was something lacking, something that she should have found missing at the first glance, yet for her life she could not have said what it was.

From below some gross omission blazed up at her, and though she was acutely aware that the scene lacked something which she had every right to expect to see, her senses groped for it in vain; although the lack of something which should have been there, and was not, was as obvious as a burning pyre at midnight. She knew that she was watching the gross defiance of some natural law, but what law she did not know. Suddenly sick and dizzy, she withdrew her head.

All the cowardice in Tessa's nature urged her to go to bed, to forget what she had seen and to refrain from trying to remember what she had *not* seen. But the other Tessa, the Tessa who despised cowards, and was herself capable under pressure of rising to great heights of courage, stayed and urged. Under her breath she talked to herself, as she always did when any crisis found her in a state of indecision.

'Tessa, you coward! How dare you be afraid! Go down at once and see who it is and what's queer about him. He can't eat you!'

So the two Tessas imprisoned in the one body stole downstairs again, and the braver Tessa was angry with their common heart for thumping so hard and trying to weaken her. But she unfastened the door and stepped out into the moonlight.

The Sweeper was still at work close to the angle of the house, near by where the path ended and a green door gave entrance to the stable yard. The path was thick with leaves, and the girl, advancing uncertainly with her hands to her breasts, saw that he was making little progress with his work. The broom rose and fell and audibly swept the path, but the dead leaves lay fast and still beneath it. Yet it was not this that she had noticed from above. There was still that unseizable Something missing.

Her footfalls made little noise on the leaf-strewn path, but they became audible to the Sweeper while she was still half a dozen yards from him. He paused in his work and turned and looked at her.

He was a tall, lean man with a white cadaverous face and eyes that bulged like huge rising bubbles as they regarded her. It was a foul, suffering face which he showed to Tessa, a face whose misery could – and did – inspire loathing and a hitherto unimagined horror, but never pity. He was clad in the meanest rags, which seemed to have been cast at random over his emaciated body. The hands grasping the broom seemed no more than bones and skin. He was so thin, thought Tessa, that he was almost – and here she paused in thought, because she found herself hating the word which tried to force itself into her mind. But it had its way, and blew in on a cold wind of terror. Yes, he was almost transparent, she thought, and sickened at the word, which had come to have a new and vile meaning for her.

They faced each other through a fraction of eternity not to be measured by seconds; and then Tessa heard herself scream. It flashed upon her now, the strange, abominable detail of the figure which confronted her – the Something missing which she had noticed, without actually seeing, from above. The path was flooded with moonlight, but the visitant had no shadow. And fast upon this vile discovery she saw dimly *through* it the ivy stirring upon the wall. Then, as unbidden thoughts rushed to tell her that the Thing was not of this world, and that it was not holy, and the sudden knowledge wrung that scream from her, so she was left suddenly and dreadfully alone. The spot where the Thing had stood was empty save for the moonlight and the shallow litter of leaves.

* * *

Tessa had no memory of returning to the house. Her next recollection was of finding herself in the hall, faint and gasping and sobbing. Even as she approached the stairs she saw a light dancing on the wall above and wondered what fresh horror was to confront her. But it was only Mrs Finch coming downstairs in a dressing-gown, candle in hand, an incongruous but a very comforting sight.

'Oh, it's you, Miss Tessa,' said Mrs Finch, reassured. She held the candle lower and peered down at the sobbing girl. 'Why, whatever is the matter? Oh, Miss Tessa, Miss Tessa! You haven't been outside, have you?'

Tessa sobbed and choked and tried to speak.

'I've seen – I've seen . . .'

Mrs Finch swiftly descended the remaining stairs, and put an arm around the shuddering girl.

'Hush, my dear, my dear! I know what you've seen. You didn't ought never to have gone out. I've seen it too, once – but only once, thank God.'

'What is it?' Tessa faltered.

'Never you mind, my dear. Now don't be frightened. It's all over now. He doesn't come here for you. It's the mistress he wants. You've nothing to fear, Miss Tessa. Where was he when you saw him?'

'Close to the end of the path, near the stable gate.'

Mrs Finch threw up her hands.

'Oh, the poor mistress – the poor mistress! Her time's shortening! The end's nigh now!'

'I can't bear any more,' Tessa sobbed; and then she contradicted herself, clinging to Mrs Finch. 'I must know. I can't rest until I know. Tell me everything.'

'Come into my parlour, my dear, and I'll make a cup of tea. We can both do with it, I think. But you'd best not know. At least not tonight, Miss Tessa – not tonight.'

'I must,' whispered Tessa, 'if I'm ever to have any peace.'

The fire was still burning behind a guard in the housekeeper's parlour, for Mrs Finch had only gone up to bed a few minutes since. There was water still warm in the brass kettle, and in a few minutes the tea was ready. Tessa sipped and felt the first vibrations of her returning courage, and presently looked inquiringly at Mrs Finch.

'I'll tell you, Miss Tessa,' said the old housekeeper, 'if it'll make you any easier. But don't let the mistress know as I've ever told you.'

Tessa inclined her head and gave the required promise.

'You don't know why,' Mrs Finch began in a low voice, 'the mistress gives to every beggar, deserving or otherwise. The reason comes into what I'm going to tell you. Miss Ludgate wasn't always like that – not until up to about fifteen years ago.

'She was old then, but active for her age, and very fond of gardenin'. Late one afternoon in the autumn, while she was cutting some late roses, a beggar came to the tradesmen's door. Sick and ill and starved, he looked – but there, you've seen him. He was a bad lot, we found out afterwards, but I was sorry for him, and I was just going to risk givin' him some food without orders, when up comes Miss Ludgate. "What's this?" she says.

'He whined something about not being able to get work.

'"Work!" says the mistress. "You don't want work – you want charity. If you want to eat," she says, "you shall, but you shall work first. There's a broom," she says, "and there's a path littered with leaves. Start sweeping up at the top, and when you come to the end you can come and see me."

'Well, he took the broom, and a few minutes later I heard a shout from Miss Ludgate and come hurryin' out. There was the man lyin' at the top of the path where he'd commenced sweeping, and he'd collapsed and fallen down. I didn't know then as he was dying, but he did, and he gave Miss Ludgate a look as I shall never forget.

'"When I've swept to the end of the path," he says, "I'll come for you, my lady, and we'll feast together. Only see as you're ready to be fetched when I come." Those were his last words. He was buried by the parish, and it gave Miss Ludgate such a turn that she ordered something to be given to every beggar who came, and not one of 'em to be asked to do a stroke of work.

'But next autumn, when the leaves began to fall, he came back and started sweeping, right at the top of the path, round about where he died. We've all heard him and most of us have seen him. Year after year he's come back and swept with his broom, which just makes a brushing noise and hardly stirs a leaf. But each year he's been getting nearer and nearer to the end of the path, and when he gets right to the end – well, I wouldn't like to be the mistress, with all her money.'

It was three evenings later, just before the hour fixed for dinner, that the Sweeper completed his task. That is to say, if one reposes literal belief in Mrs Finch's story.

The servants heard somebody burst open the tradesmen's door, and, having rushed out into the passage, two of them saw that the door was open but found no one there. Miss Ludgate was already in the drawing-room, but Tessa was still upstairs, dressing for dinner. Presently Mrs Finch had occasion to enter the drawing-room to speak to her mistress; and her screams warned the household of what had happened. Tessa heard them just as she was ready to go downstairs, and she rushed into the drawing-room a few moments later.

Miss Ludgate was sitting upright in her favourite chair. Her eyes were open, but she was quite dead; and in her eyes there was something that Tessa could not bear to see.

Withdrawing her own gaze from that fixed stare of terror and recognition she saw something on the carpet and presently stooped to pick it up.

It was a little yellow leaf, damp and pinched and frayed, and but for her own experience and Mrs Finch's tale she might have wondered how it had come to be there. She dropped it, shuddering, for it looked as if it had been picked up by, and had afterwards fallen from, the birch twigs of a stable broom.

The Boys' Toilets
Robert Westall

The January term started with a scene of sheer disaster. A muddy excavator was chewing its way across the netball-court, breakfasting on the tarmac with sinuous lunges and terrifying swings of its yellow dinosaur neck. One of the stone balls had been knocked off the gate-posts, and lay in crushed fragments, like a Malteser trodden on by a giant. The entrance to the science wing was blocked with a pile of ochreous clay, and curved glazed drainpipes were heaped like school dinners' macaroni.

The girls hung round in groups. One girl came back from the indoor toilets saying Miss Bowker was phoning the Council, and using words that Eliza Bottom had nearly been expelled for last term. She was greeted with snorts of disbelief . . .

The next girl came back from the toilet saying Miss Bowker was nearly crying.

Which was definitely a lie, because here was Miss Bowker now, come out to address them in her best sheepskin coat. Though she *was* wearing fresh make-up, and her eyes were suspiciously bright, her famous chin was up. She was brief, and to the point. There was an underground leak in the central heating; till it was mended, they would be using the old Harvest Road boys' school. They would march across now, by forms, in good order, in charge of the prefects. She knew they would behave immaculately, and that the spirit of Spilsby Girls' Grammar would overcome all difficulties . . .

'Take more than school spirit,' said Wendy Falstaff.

'More than a bottle of whisky,' said Jennifer Mount, and shuddered. Rebeccah, who was a vicar's daughter, thought of Sodom and Gomorrah; both respectable suburbs by comparison with Harvest Road. Harvest Road was literally on the wrong side of the tracks. But obediently they marched. They passed through the streets where they lived, gay with yellow front doors, picture-windows, new carports and wrought-iron gates. It was quite an adventure at first. Staff cars kept passing them, their rear-windows packed with whole classrooms. Miss Rossiter, with her brass microscopes and stuffed ducks; Mademoiselle, full of tape-recorders and posters of the French wine-growing districts. Piles of *The Merchant of Venice* and 'Sunflowers' by Van Gogh . . .

The first time they passed, the teachers hooted cheerfully. But coming back they were silent, just their winkers winking, and frozen faces behind the wheel.

Then the marching columns came to a miserable little hump-backed bridge over a solitary railway-line, empty and rusting. Beyond were the same kind of houses; but afflicted by some dreadful disease, of which the symptoms were a rash of small window-panes, flaking paint, overgrown funereal privet-hedges and sagging gates that would never shut again. And then it seemed to grow colder still, as the slum-clearances started, a great empty plain of broken brick, and the wind hit them full, sandpapering faces and sending grey berets cartwheeling into the wilderness.

And there, in the midst of the desolation, like a dead sooty dinosaur, like a blackened, marooned, many-chimneyed Victorian battleship, lay Harvest Road school.

They gathered, awed, in the hall. The windows, too high up to see out of, were stained brown round the edges; the walls were dark-green. There was a carved oak board, a list of prize-winners from 1879 till 1923. Victoria peered at it. 'It's BC, not AD,' she announced. 'The first name's

Tutankhamun.' There were posters sagging off the walls, on the extreme ends of long hairy strands of sticky tape; things like "Tea-picking in India" and "The Meaning of Empire Day". It all felt rather like drowning in a very dirty goldfish tank.

A lot of them wanted the toilet, badly. Nervousness and the walk through the cold. But nobody felt like asking till Rebeccah did. Last door at the end of the corridor and across the yard; they walked down, six-strong.

They were boys' toilets. They crept past the male mystery of the urinals, tall, white and rust-streaked as tombs, looking absurd, inhuman, like elderly invalid-carriages or artificial limbs. In the bottom gulley, fag-ends lay squashed and dried-out, like dead flies.

And the graffiti . . . even Liza Bottom didn't know what some words meant. But they were huge and hating . . . the whole wall screamed with them, from top to bottom. Most of the hate seemed directed at someone called "Barney Boko".

Rebeccah shuddered; that was the first shudder. But Vicky only said practically 'Bet there's no toilet-paper!' and got out her French exercise-book . . . She was always the pessimist; but on this occasion she hadn't been pessimistic enough. Not only no toilet-paper, but no wooden seats either, and the lavatory-chains had been replaced by loops of hairy thick white string, like hangmen's nooses. And in the green paint of the wooden partitions, the hatred of Barney Boko had been gouged half-an-inch deep. And the locks had been bust off all the doors except the far end one . . .

Rebeccah, ever public-spirited and with a lesser need, stood guard stoutly without.

'Boys,' she heard Victoria snort in disgust. 'It's a nunnery for me . . . at least in nunneries they'll have soft toilet-paper.'

'Don't you believe it,' said Joanne, their Roman Catholic correspondent. 'They wear hair-shirts, nuns. Probably the toilets have *scrubbing-brushes* instead of paper.'

Lively squeaks, all down the line, as the implications struck home.

'Some boys aren't bad,' said Liza, 'if you can get them away from their friends.'

'Why bother,' said Vicky. 'I'll settle for my poster of Duran Duran . . .'

'It's funny,' said Tracy, as they were combing their hair in the solitary cracked, fly-spotted, pocket-handkerchief-sized mirror. 'You know there's six of us? Well, I heard *seven* toilets flush. Did anybody pull the chain twice?'

They all looked at each other, and shook their heads. They looked back down the long shadowy loo, with its tiny, high-up pebbled windows, towards the toilets. They shouted, wanting to know who was there, because nobody had passed them, nobody had come in.

No answer, except the sound of dripping.

The big attraction at break was the school boiler-house. They stood round on the immense coke-heaps, some new, some so old and mixed with the fallen leaves of many autumns they were hardly recognisable as coke at all. One actually had weeds growing on it . . .

Inside the boiler-house, in a red hissing glow, two men fought to get Harvest Road up to a reasonable temperature, somewhere above that of Dracula's crypt. One was young, cheerful, cocky, with curly brown hair; they said he was from the Council. The other was tall and thin, in a long grey overall-coat and cap so old the pattern had worn off. They said he was the caretaker of the old school, brought out of retirement because only he knew the ropes . . . he had such an expression on his face that they immediately called him Dracula. Occasionally, the cocky one would stop shovelling coke into the gaping red maw of the furnace and wipe his brow; that, and the occasional draught of warm air, immediately swept away by the biting wind, was the only hint of heat they had that morning.

The lesson after break was maths, with Miss Hogg. Miss Hogg was one of the old school; grey hair in a tight bun, tweeds, gold-rimmed spectacles. A brilliant mathematician who had once unbent far enough, at the end of summer term, to tell the joke about the square on the hypotenuse. Feared but not loved, Miss Hogg made it quite clear to all that she had no time for men.

They ground away steadily at quadratic equations, until the dreary cold, seeping out of the tiled walls into their bones, claimed Rebeccah as its first victim. Her hand shot up.

'You should have gone at break,' said Miss Hogg.

'I did, Miss Hogg.'

Miss Hogg's gesture gave permission, while despairing of all the fatal weaknesses of femininity.

Rebeccah hesitated just inside the doorway of the loo. The length of the low dark room, vanishing into shadow; the little green windows high up that lit nothing, the alienness of it all made her hesitant, as in some old dark church. The graffiti plucked at the corners of her eyes, dimly, like memorials on a church wall. But no 'dearly beloveds' here.

JACKO IS A SLIMER
HIGGINS STINKS

Where were they now? How many years ago? She told herself they must be grown men, balding, with wives and families and little paunches under cardigans their wives had lovingly knitted for them. But she couldn't believe it. They were still here somewhere, fighting, snorting bubbles of blood from streaming noses, angry. Especially angry with Barney Boko. She went down the long room on tiptoe, and went into the far-end toilet because it was the only one with a lock. Snapped home the bolt so hard it echoed up and down the concrete ceiling.

But no sooner had she settled than she heard someone come in. Not a girl; Rebeccah had quick ears. No, big boots, with steel heel-plates. Walking authoritatively towards her. From the liveliness of the feet she knew it wasn't even a man. A boy. She heard him pause, as if he sensed her; as if looking round. Then, a boy's voice, quiet.

'OK, Stebbo, all clear!'

More stamping heel-capped feet tramping in.

She knew she had made a terrible mistake. There must still be a boys' school here; only occupying part of the buildings. And she was in the *boys'* loo. She blushed. An enormous blush that seemed to start behind her ears, and went down her neck over her whole body . . .

But she was a sensible child. She told herself to be calm. Just sit, quiet as a mouse till they'd gone. She sat, breathing softly into her handkerchief, held across her mouth.

But supposing they tried the door, shouted to know who was in there? Suppose they put their hands on the top of the wooden partition and hauled themselves up and looked over the top. There were some awful *girls* who did that . . .

But they seemed to have no interest in her locked cubicle. There was a lot of scuffling, a scraping of steel heel-plates and a panting. As if they were dragging somebody . . .

The somebody was dragged into the cubicle next door. Elbows thumped against the wooden partition, making her jump.

'Get his head down,' ordered a sharp voice.

'No, Stebbo NO! Let me go, you bastards . . .'

'Ouch!'

'What's up?'

'Little sod bit me . . .'

'Get his head down then!'

The sounds of heaving, scraping, panting, and finally a sort of high-pitched whining, got worse. Then suddenly the toilet next door flushed, the whining stopped, then resumed as a series of half-drowned gasps for breath. There was a yip of triumph, laughter, and the noise of many boots running away.

'Bastards,' said a bitter, choking voice. 'And you've broken my pen an' all.' Then a last weary pair of boots trailed away.

She got herself ready, listening, waiting, tensed. Then undid the bolt with a rush and ran down the empty echoing place. Her own footsteps sounded frail and tiny, after the boys. Suppose she met one, coming in?

But she didn't. And there wasn't a boy in sight in the grey high-walled yard. Bolder, she looked back at the entrance of the loo . . . it was the same one they'd used earlier; the one they'd been told to use. Miss Bowker must have made a mistake; someone should be told . . .

But when she got back to the classroom, and Miss Hogg and all the class looked up, she lost her nerve.

'You took your time, Rebeccah,' said Miss Hogg, suspiciously.

'We thought you'd pulled the chain too soon and gone down to the sea-side,' said Liza Bottom, playing for a vulgar laugh and getting it.

'Let me see your work so far, Liza,' said Miss Hogg frostily, killing the laughter like a partridge shot on the wing.

'What's up?' whispered Vicky. 'You met a fellah or something – all blushing and eyes shining . . .' Vicky was much harder to fool than Miss Hogg.

'Tell you at lunch . . .'

'The next girl I see talking . . .' said Miss Hogg ominously.

But they didn't have to wait till lunch. Liza had twigged that something was up. Her hand shot up; she squirmed in her seat almost too convincingly.

'Very well, Liza. I suppose I must brace myself for an epidemic of weak bladders . . .'

Liza returned like a bomb about to explode, her ginger hair standing out from her head like she'd back-combed it for Saturday night, a deep blush under her freckles and green eyes wide as saucers. She opened her mouth to speak . . . but Miss Hogg had an eagle eye for incipient hysteria, and a gift for nipping it in the bud.

'Shut the door, Liza, we'll keep the draughts we have.' Liza sat down demurely; but even the Hogg's frost couldn't stop the idea flaring across the class that something was excitingly amiss in the loos. It was droopy Margie Trawson who blew it. She went next; and came back and bleated, with that air of a victimised sheep that only she could achieve.

'Miss, there's boys in the toilet . . .'

'Boys?' boomed Miss Hogg. 'BOYS?' She swept out of the classroom door with all the speed her strongly-muscled legs could give her. From the classroom windows, they watched as she entered the toilets. Rebeccah, who was rather keen on naval warfare in World War II, thought she looked like an angry little frigate, just itching to depth-charge any boy out of existence. But when she emerged, her frown told that she'd been cheated of her prey. She scouted on for boys lurking behind the coke-heaps, behind the dustbins, behind the sagging fence of the caretaker's house. Nothing. She looked back towards her classroom windows, making every girlish head duck simultaneously, then headed for the Headmistress's office.

In turn, they saw the tall stately figure of the Head inspect the loo, the coke-heaps, fence and dustbins, Miss Hogg circling her on convoy-duty. But without success. Finally, after a word, they parted. Miss Hogg returned, with a face like thunder.

'Someone,' she announced, 'has been silly. Very, *very*, silly.' She made 'silly' sound as evil as running a concentration camp. 'The Head has assured me that this school has been disused for many years, and there cannot possibly be a single boy on the premises. The only . . . males . . . are the caretakers. Now, Margie, what have you got to say to *that*? Well . . . Margie . . . *well*?'

There was only one end to Miss Hogg's well-Margie-well routine. Margie gruesomely dissolving into tears. 'There were boys, Miss, I heard them, Miss, honeeest . . .' She pushed back a tear with the cuff of her cardigan.

Liza was on her feet, flaming. 'I heard them too, Miss.' That didn't worry Miss Hogg. Liza was the form trouble-maker. But then Rebeccah was on her feet. 'I heard them as well.'

'*Rebeccah* – you are a clergyman's daughter. I'm ashamed of you.'

'I *heard* them.' Rebeccah clenched her teeth; there would be no shifting her. Miss Hogg looked thoughtful.

'They don't come when you're in a crowd, Miss,' bleated Margie. 'They only come when you're there by yourself. They put another boy's head down the toilet an' pulled the chain. They were in the place next to me.'

'And to me,' said Liza.

'And to me,' said Rebeccah.

A sort of shiver went round the class; the humming and buzzing stopped, and it was very quiet.

'Very well,' said Miss Hogg. 'We will test Margie's theory. *Come*, Rebeccah!'

At the entrance to the toilet, Rebeccah suddenly felt very silly.

'Just go in and behave normally,' said Miss Hogg. 'I shall be just outside.'

Rebeccah entered the toilet, bolted the door and sat down.

'Do exactly what you would normally do,' boomed Miss Hogg, suddenly, scarily, down the long dark space. Rebeccah blushed again, and did as she was told.

'There,' boomed Miss Hogg, after a lengthy pause. 'Nothing, you see. Nothing at all. You girls are *ridiculous*!' Rebeccah wasn't so sure. There was something – you couldn't call it a sound – a sort of vibration in the air, like boys giggling in hiding.

'Nothing,' boomed Miss Hogg again. 'Come along – we've wasted enough lesson-time. Such nonsense.'

Suddenly a toilet flushed, at the far end of the row.

'Was that you, Rebeccah?'

'No, Miss Hogg.'

'Rubbish. Of course it was.'

'No, Miss.'

Another toilet flushed; and another; getting nearer. That convinced Miss Hogg. Rebeccah heard her stout brogues come in at a run, heard her banging back the toilet-doors, shouting,

'Come out, whoever you are. You can't get away. I know you're there.'

Rebeccah came out with a rush to meet her.

'Did you pull your chain, Rebeccah?'

'Didn't need to, Miss.'

And indeed, all the toilet doors were now open, and all the toilets manifestly empty, and every cistern busy refilling; except Rebeccah's.

'There must be a scientific explanation,' said Miss Hogg. 'A fault in the plumbing.'

But Rebeccah thought she heard a quiver in her voice, as she stared suspiciously at the small, inaccessible ventilation grids.

They all went together at lunchtime; and nothing happened. They all went together at afternoon break, and nothing happened. Then it was time for Miss Hogg again. Black Monday was called Black Monday because they had Miss Hogg twice for Maths.

And still the cold worked upon their systems . . .

Margie Trawson again.

'Please, Miss, I *got* to.'

Only . . . there was a secret in Margie's voice, a little gloaty secret. They all heard it; but if Miss Hogg did, she only raised a grizzled eyebrow. 'Hurry, then . . . if only your *mind* was so active, Margie.'

She was gone a long time; a very long time. Even Miss Hogg shifted her brogued feet restlessly, as she got on with marking the other third-year form's quadratic equations.

And then Margie was standing in the doorway, and behind her, the looming grey-coated figure of Dracula, with his mouth set so hard and cruel. He had Margie by the elbow, in a grip that made her writhe. He whispered to Miss Hogg . . .

'Appalling,' boomed Miss Hogg. 'I don't know what these children think they are coming to. Thank you for telling me so quickly, caretaker. It won't happen again. I assure you, it won't happen again. That will be all!'

Dracula, robbed of his moment of public triumph and infant-humiliation, stalked out without another word.

'Margie,' announced Miss Hogg, 'has attempted to use the caretaker's outside toilet. The toilet set aside for his own personal use. A *man's* toilet . . .'

'Obviously a hanging offence,' muttered Victoria, causing a wild but limited explosion of giggles, cut off as by a knife, by Miss Hogg's glint-spectacled *look*. 'How would you like it, Margie, if some strange men came into your backyard at home and used *your* toilet?'

'It'd really turn her on,' muttered Victoria. Liza choked down on a giggle so hard, she nearly gave herself a slipped disc.

'No girl will ever do such a thing again,' said Miss Hogg in her most dreadful voice, clutching Margie's elbow as cruelly as Dracula had. A voice so dreadful and so seldom heard that the whole form froze into thoughtfulness. Not since that joke with the chewing-gum in the first year had they heard *that* voice.

'Now, Margie, will you go and do what you have to do, in the place where you are meant to do it.'

'Don't want to go no more, Miss. It's gone off . . .'

Liar, thought Rebeccah; Margie needed to go so badly, she was squirming from foot to foot.

'GO!' said Miss Hogg, in the voice that brooked no argument. 'I shall watch you from the window.'

They all watched her go in; and they all watched her come out.

'Sit down quickly, Margie,' said Miss Hogg. 'There seems to be some difficulty with question twelve. It's quite simple really.' She turned away to the blackboard, chalk in hand. 'x squared, plus 2y . . .' The chalk squeaked abominably, getting on everyone's nerves; there was a slight but growing disturbance at the back of the class, which Miss Hogg couldn't hear for the squeaking of the chalk . . . '3x plus 5y' . . .

'Oh, *Miss*!' wailed Margie. 'I'm sorry, Miss . . . I didn't mean to . . .' Then she was flying to the classroom door, babbling and sobbing incoherently. She scrabbled for the door-knob and finally got it open. Miss Hogg moved across swiftly and tried to grab her, but she was just too slow; Margie was gone, with Miss Hogg in hot pursuit, hysterical sobs and angry shouts echoing round the whole school from the pair of them.

'What . . .?' asked Rebeccah, turning. Vicky pointed silently, at a wide spreading pool of liquid under Margie's desk.

'She never went at all,' said Vicky grimly. 'She must have hidden just inside the loo doorway. She was too scared . . .'

It was then that Rebeccah began to hate the ghosts in the boys' toilets.

She tapped on Dad's study door, as soon as she got in from school. Pushed it open. He was sitting, a tall thin boyish figure, at his desk with the desk-light on. From his dejectedly drooping shoulders, and his spectacles pushed up on his forehead, she knew he was writing next Sunday's sermon. He was bashing between his eyes with a balled fist as well; Epiphany was never his favourite topic for a sermon.

'Dad?'

He came back from far away, pulled down his spectacles, blinked at her and smiled.

'It's the Person from Porlock!' This was a very ancient joke between them, that only got better with time. The real Person from Porlock had interrupted the famous poet Coleridge, when he was in the middle of composing his greatest poem, 'Kubla Khan'.

'Sit down, Person,' said Dad, removing a precarious tower of books from his second wooden armchair. 'Want a coffee?' She glanced at his percolator; shiny and new from Mum last Christmas, but now varnished-over with dribbles, from constant use.

'Yes please,' she said, just to be matey; he made his coffee as strong as poison.

'How's Porlock?' He gave her a sharp sideways glance through his horn-rimmed spectacles. 'Trouble?'

Somehow, he always knew.

She was glad she could start at the beginning, with ordinary things like the central heating and the march to Harvest Road . . .

When she had finished, he said, 'Ghosts. Ghosts in the toilet. Pulling chains and frightening people.' He was the only adult she knew who wouldn't have laughed or made some stupid remark. But all he said was, 'Something funny happened at that school. It was closed down. A few years before Mum and I came to live here. It had an evil name; but I never knew for what.'

'But what can we *do*? The girls are terrified.'

'Go at lunchtime – go at break – go before you leave home.'

'We do. But it's so cold – somebody'll get caught out sooner or later.'

'You won't be at Harvest Road long – even central heating leaks don't go on for ever. Shall I try to find out how long? I know the Chairman of Governors.'

'Wouldn't do any harm,' said Rebeccah grudgingly.

'But you don't want to wait to go that long?' It was meant to be a joke; but it died halfway between them.

'Look,' said Rebeccah, 'if you'd seen Margie . . . she . . . she won't dare come back. Somebody could be . . . terrified for life.'

'I'll talk to your Headmistress . . .' He reached for the phone.

'NO!' It came out as nearly a shout. Dad put the phone back, looking puzzled. Rebeccah said, in a low voice,

'The teachers think we're nuts. They'll . . . think you're nuts as well. You . . . can't afford to have people think *you're* nuts. Can you?'

'Touché,' he said ruefully. 'So what do you want, Person?'

'Tell me how to get rid of them. How to frighten them away, so they leave people *alone*.'

'I'm not in the frightening business, Person.'

'But the church . . .'

'You mean . . . bell, book and candle? No can do. The church doesn't like that kind of thing any more . . . doesn't believe in it, I suppose . . .'

'But it's *real*.' It was almost a wail.

'The only man I know who touches that sort of thing has a parish in London. He's considered a crank.'

'*Tell me what to do!*'

They looked at each other in silence, a very long time. They were so much alike, with their blonde hair, long faces, straight noses, spectacles. Even their hair was the same length; he wore his long; she wore hers shortish.

Finally he said, 'There's no other way?'

'No.'

'I don't know much. You're supposed to ask its name. It has to tell you – that's in the Bible. That's supposed to give you power over it. Then, like Shakespeare, you can ask it whether it's a spirit of health or goblin damned. Then . . . you can try commanding it to go to the place prepared for it . . .' He jumped up, running his fingers through his hair. 'No, you mustn't do any of this, Rebeccah. I can't have you doing things like this. I'll ring the Head . . .'

'You will NOT!'

'Leave it alone, then!'

'If it lets me alone.' But she had her fingers crossed.

* * *

The Head came in to address them next morning, after assembly. She put her hands together behind her back, rocked a little, head down, then looked at them with a smile that was a hundred per cent caring, and about ninety per cent honest.

'Toilets,' she said doubtfully, then with an effort, more briskly, 'Toilets.' She nodded gently. 'I can understand you are upset about the toilets. Of all the things about this dreadful place that the Council's put us in, those toilets are the worst. I want you to know that I have had the strongest possible words with the Council, and that those toilets will be repainted and repaired by next Monday morning. I have told them that if they fail me in this, I will close the school.' She lowered her head in deep thought again, then looked up, more sympathetic than ever.

'You have reached an age when you are – quite rightly – beginning to be interested in boys. There *have* been boys here – they have left their mark – and I am sad they have left the worst possible kind of mark. Most boys are not like that – not like that at all, thank God. But – these boys have been *gone* for over twenty years. Let me stress that. For twenty years, this building has been used to store unwanted school furniture. You may say that there are always boys everywhere – like mice, or beetles! But with all this slum-clearance around us . . . I went out yesterday actually *looking* for a boy.' She looked round with a smile, expecting a laugh. She got a few titters. 'The first boy I saw was a full mile away – and he was working for a butcher in the High Street.' Again, she expected a laugh, and it did not come. So she went serious again. 'You have been upset by the toilets – understandably. But that is no excuse for making things up – for, and I must say it, getting hysterical. Nobody else has noticed anything in these toilets. The prefects report nothing –

I have watched first and second years using them quite happily. *It is just this class.* Or rather, three excitable girls in this class . . .' She looked round. At Liza Bottom, who blushed and wriggled. At the empty desk where Margie should have been sitting. And at Rebeccah, who stared straight back at her, as firmly as she could. 'Two of those girls do not surprise me – the third girl does.' Rebeccah did not flinch, which worried the Head, who was rather fond of her. So the Head finished in rather a rush. 'I want you to stop acting as feather-brained females – and act instead as the sensible, hard-headed young women you are going to become. This business . . . is the sort of business that gets us despised by men . . . and there are plenty of men only too ready to despise us.'

The Head swept out. A sort of deadly coldness settled over the sensible young women. It hadn't happened to the prefects, or to the first years. The Head had just proved there were ghosts, and proved they were only after people in 3A . . .

It was Fiona Mowbray who bought it. It happened so swiftly, after break. They'd all gone together at break. They never realized they'd left her there, too shy to call out. She was always the shyest, Fiona . . .

Suddenly she appeared in the doorway, interrupting the beginning of French.

'Sit down, Feeownah,' said Mamselle, gently.

But Fiona just stood there, pale and stiff as a scarecrow, swaying. There were strange twists of toilet-paper all round her arms . . .

'Feeownah,' said Mamselle again with a strange panicky quiver in her voice. Fiona opened and closed her mouth to speak four times, without a single sound coming out. Then she fainted full-length, hitting the floorboard like a sack of potatoes.

Then someone ran for the Head, and everyone was crowding round, and the Head was calling stand back give her air and sending Liza for Miss Hogg's smelling salts. And Fiona coming round and starting to scream and flail out. And fainting again. And talk of sending for a doctor . . .

Right, you sod, thought Rebeccah. That's *it*! And she slipped round the back of the clustering crowd, and nobody saw her go, for all eyes were on Fiona.

Fiona must have been in the third toilet . . . the toilet-roll holder was empty, and the yellow paper, swathe on swathe of it, covered the floor and almost buried the lavatory-bowl. It was wildly torn in places, as if Fiona had had to claw her way out of it. Had it . . . been trying to smother her? Rebeccah pulled the chain automatically. Then, with a wildly-beating heart, locked herself in the next door, and sat down with her jaw clenched and her knickers round her knees.

It was hard to stay calm. The noise of the refilling cistern next door hid all other noises. Then, as next door dropped to a trickle, she heard another toilet being pulled. Had someone else come in, unheard? Was she wasting her time? But there'd been no footsteps. Then another toilet flushed, and another and another. Then the doors of the empty toilets began banging, over and over, so hard and savagely that she thought they must splinter.

Boom, boom, boom. Nearer and nearer.

Come on, bastard, thought Rebeccah, with the hard centre of her mind; the rest of her felt like screaming.

Then the toilet pulled over her own head. So violently it showered her with water. She looked up, and the hairy string was swinging, with no one holding it . . . like a hangman's noose. Nobody could possibly have touched it.

The cistern-lever was pulled above her, again and again. Her nerve broke, and she rushed for the door. But the bolt wouldn't unbolt. Too stiff – too stiff for her terrified fingers. She flung herself round wildly, trying to climb over the top, but she was so terrified she couldn't manage that, either. She ended up cowering down against the door, head on her knees and hands over her ears, like an unborn baby.

Silence. Stillness. But she knew that whatever it was, it was still there.

'What . . . is . . . your . . . name?' she whispered, from a creaky throat. Then a shout. 'WHAT IS YOUR NAME?'

As if in answer, the toilet-roll began to unroll itself, rearing over her in swirling yellow coils, as if it wanted to smother her.

'Are you a spirit of health or goblin damned?' That reminded her of Dad, and gave her a little chip of courage. But the folds of paper went on rearing up, till all the cubicle was filled with the yellow, rustling mass. As if you had to *breathe* toilet paper.

'Begone . . . to the place . . . prepared for you,' she stammered, without hope. The coils of paper moved nearer, touching her face softly.

'WHAT DO YOU WANT?' She was screaming.

There was a change. The whirling folds of paper seemed to coalesce. Into a figure, taller than herself, as tall as a very thin boy might be, wrapped in yellow bands like a mummy, with two dark gaps where eyes might have been.

If it had touched her, her mind would have splintered into a thousand pieces.

But it didn't. It just looked at her, with its hole-eyes, and swung a yellow-swathed scarecrow arm to point to the brickwork above the cistern.

Three times. Till she dumbly nodded.

Then it collapsed into a mass of paper round her feet.

After a long time, she got up and tried the doorbolt. It opened easily, and her fear changed to embarrassment as she grabbed for her pants.

It hadn't wanted to harm her at all; it had only wanted to show her something.

Emboldened, she waded back through the yellow mass. Where had it been pointing?

There could be no mistake; a tiny strand of toilet-paper still clung to the brickwork, caught in a crack. She pulled it out, and the white paintwork crumbled a little and came with it, leaving a tiny hole. She touched the part near the hole, and more paint and cement crumbled; she scrabbled, and a whole half-brick seemed to fall out into her hand. Only it wasn't all brick, but crumbly dried mud, which broke and fell in crumbs all over the yellow paper.

What a mess! But left exposed was a square black hole, and there was something stuck inside. She reached in, and lifted down a thick bundle of papers . . .

Something made her lock the door, sit down on the toilet, and pull them out of their elastic band, which snapped with age as she touched it. Good heavens . . . her mouth dropped open, appalled.

There was a dusty passport; and a wallet. The wallet was full of money, notes. Pound notes and French thousand-franc notes. And a driving-licence, made out in the name of a Mr Alfred Barnett. And letters to Mr Barnett. And tickets for trains and a cross-channel ferry . . . and the passport, dated to expire on the first of April 1958, was also made out in the name of Alfred and Ada Barnett . . .

She sat there, and church-child that she was, she cried a little with relief and the pity of it. The ghost was a boy who had stolen and hidden the loot, so well concealed, all those years ago. And after he was dead, he was sorry, and wanted to make amends. But the school was abandoned by then; no one to listen to him; old Dracula would never listen to a poor lost ghost . . . well, she would make amends for him, and then he would be at rest, poor lonely thing.

She looked at the address in the passport. 'Briardene', 12 Millbrook Gardens, Spilsby . . . why, it was only ten minutes' walk; she could do it on her way home tonight, and they wouldn't even worry about her getting home a bit late.

She was still sitting there in a happy and pious daze at the virtue of the universe, when faithful Vicky came looking for her. Only faithful Vicky had noticed she was gone. So she told her, and Vicky said she would come as well . . .

'They've taken Fiona to hospital . . .'

Perhaps that should have been a warning; but Rebeccah was too happy. 'She'll get over it; and once we've taken this, it won't hurt anybody else again.'

It all seemed so simple.

Liza came too; out of sheer nosiness, but Rebeccah was feeling charitable to all the world. It was that kind of blessed evening you sometimes get in January, lovely and bright, that makes you think of spring before the next snow falls.

Millbrook Gardens was in an older, solider district than their own; posher in its funny old way. Walls of brick that glowed a deep rich red in the setting sun, and showed their walking, blue girlish shadows, where there wasn't any ivy or the bare strands of Virginia Creeper. So it seemed that dim ghosts walked with them, among the houses with their white iron conservatories and old trees with homemade swings, and garden-seats still damp from winter. And funny stuffy names like 'Lynfield' and 'Spring

Lodge' and 'Nevsky Villa'. It was hard to find 'Briardene'. There were no numbers on the houses. But they found it at last, looked over the gate and saw a snowy-haired, rosy-cheeked old man turning over the rose-beds in the big front garden.

He was quite a way from the gate; but he turned and looked at them. It wasn't a nice look; a long examining unfriendly look. They felt he didn't like children; they felt he would have liked to stop them coming in. But when Rebeccah called, in a too-shrill voice, 'Do Barnetts live here?' he abruptly waved them through to the front door, and went back to his digging. Rebeccah thought he must be the gardener; his clothes were quite old and shabby.

They trooped up to the front door, and rang. There was no answer for quite a long time, then the image of a plump, white-haired woman swam up the dark hall, all broken up by the stained-glass in the door.

She looked a bit friendlier than the gardener, but not much; full of an ancient suspicion and wariness.

'Yes, children?' she said, in an old-fashioned bossy way.

Rebeccah held out her dusty package, proudly. 'We found this – I think it's yours . . .'

The woman took it from her briskly enough; the way you take a parcel off a postman. But when she began to take off Rebeccah's new elastic band, she suddenly looked so . . . as if she'd like to drop the packet and slam the door.

'It's a passport and money and tickets and things,' said Rebeccah helpfully.

The woman put a hand to her eyes, to shield them as if the sunlight was too strong; she nearly fell, leaning against the door-post just in time. 'Alfred,' she called, 'Alfred!' to the man in the garden. Then Rebeccah knew the man was her husband, and she thought the cry was almost a call for help. As if they'd been attacking the woman . . .

The old man came hurrying up, full of petty anger at being disturbed. Until his wife handed him the packet. Then he too seemed to shrink, shrivel. The healthy high colour fled his cheeks, leaving only a pattern of bright broken veins, as if they'd been drawn on wrinkled fish-skin with a red Biro.

'They're . . .' said the woman.

'Yes,' said the man. Then he turned on the girls so fiercely they nearly ran away. His eyes were little and black and so full of hate that they, who had never been hit in their lives, grew afraid of being hit.

'*Where did you get these?*' There was authority in the voice, an ancient cruel utter authority . . .

'At Harvest Road School . . . I found them in the boys' toilets . . . hidden behind a whitewashed brick . . .'

'*Which toilet?*' The old man had grabbed Rebeccah with a terrible strength, by the shoulders; his fingers were savage. He began to shake her.

'Ey, watch it,' said Liza, aggressively. 'There's a law against that kind of thing.'

'I think we'll go now,' said Vicky frostily.

'*Which toilet?*'

'The far end one,' Rebeccah managed to gasp out. Staring into the old man's hot mad eyes, she was really frightened. This was not the way she'd meant things to go at all.

'*How* did you find it?' And, 'What were *you* doing there?'

'We're using the school . . . till ours is mended . . . we have to use the boys' toilets . . .'

'*Who* showed you?' Under his eyes, Rebeccah thought she was starting to fall to bits. Was he a lost member of the Gestapo, the Waffen SS? So she cried out, which she hadn't meant to,

'A *ghost* showed me – the ghost of a boy. It pointed to it . . .'

'That's right,' said Liza, 'there *was* a ghost.' Stubbornly, loyally.

It worked; another terrible change came over the old man. All the cruel strength flowed out of his fingers. His face went whiter than ever. He staggered, and clutched at the windowsill to support himself. He began to breathe in a rather terrifying loud unnatural way.

'Help me get him in,' cried the woman. 'Help me get him in quick.'

Heaving and straining and panting and slithering on the dark polished floor, they got him through the hall and into a chintz armchair by the fire. He seemed to go unconscious. The woman went out, and came back with a tablet that she slipped into his mouth. He managed to swallow it. At first his breathing did not alter; then slowly it began to become more normal.

The woman seemed to come to herself; become aware of the little crowd, watching wide-eyed and gape-mouthed what they knew was a struggle between life and death.

'He'll be all right now,' she said doubtfully. 'You'd better be off home, children, before your mothers start to worry.' At the door she said, 'Thank you for bringing the things – I'm sure you thought you were doing your best.' She did not sound at all thankful really.

'We thought you'd better have them,' said Rebeccah politely. 'Even though they were so old . . .'

The woman looked sharply at her, as she heard the question in her voice. 'I suppose you'll want to tell your Headmistress what happened? You should have handed in the stuff to her, really . . . well, Mr Barnett was the last headmaster of Harvest Road – when it was boys, I mean – a secondary modern. It happened – those things were stolen on the last day of the summer term. We were going on holiday in France next day . . . we never went, we couldn't. My husband knew the boy who had stolen them, but he couldn't prove it. He had the school searched from top to bottom . . . the boy would admit nothing. It broke my husband's health . . . he resigned soon after, when the school had to close . . . good night, children. Thank you.'

She went as if to close the door on them, but Liza said sharply, 'Did the boys call your husband Barney Boko?'

The woman gave a slight but distinct shudder, though it could have been the cold January evening. 'Yes . . . they were cruel days, those, cruel.'

Then she closed the door quickly, leaving them standing there.

They hadn't gone fifty yards when Liza stopped them, grabbing each of them frantically by the arm, as if she was having a fit or something.

'Don't have it here,' said Vicky sharply. 'Wait till we get you to the hospital!'

But Liza didn't laugh. 'I remember now,' she said. 'Listen – my Dad went to that school – it was a terrible place. Barney Boko – Dad said he caned the kids for everything – even for spelling mistakes. The kids really hated him – some parents tried to go to the Governors an' the Council, but it didn't do any good. There was a boy called Stebbing – Barney Boko caned him once too often – he was found dead. I think it might have been in them toilets. The verdict was he fell – he had one of those thin skulls or something. They said he fell and banged his head.'

They stared at each other in horror.

'D'you think Stebbing's . . . what's in the toilets now?' asked Vicky.

They glanced round the empty streets; the lovely sun had vanished, and it had got dark awfully suddenly. There was a sudden rush coming at them round the corner – a ghostly rustling rush – but it was only long-dead autumn leaves, driven by the wind.

'Yes,' said Rebeccah, as calmly as she could. 'I think it was Stebbing. But he hasn't got anything against *us* – we did what he wanted.'

'What *did* he want?' asked Vicky.

'For me to take back what he'd stolen – to make up for the wrong he did.'

'You're too good for this world, Rebeccah!'

'What you mean?'

'Did Stebbing *feel* like he was sorry?' asked Vicky. 'Making Margie wet herself? Frightening Fiona into a fit? What he did to *you*?'

Rebeccah shuddered. 'He was angry . . .'

'What we have just seen,' said Vicky, 'is Stebbing's revenge . . .'

'How horrible. I don't believe that – it's too horrible . . .'

'He used you, ducky . . . boys will, if you let them . . .' Vicky sounded suddenly terribly bitter.

'Oh, I'm not going to listen. I'm going home.'

They parted in a bad silent mood with each other, though they stayed together as long as they could, through the windy streets, where the pools of light from the street-lights swayed. Rebeccah had the worst journey; she took her usual short-cut through the churchyard; before she'd realised what she'd done, she was halfway across and there was no point in turning back. She stood paralysed, staring at the teeth-like ranks of tombstones, that grinned at her in the faintest light of the last street-lamp.

Somewhere, among them, Stebbing must be buried. And the worst of it was, the oldest, Victorian gravestones were behind her, and the newer ones in front. She could just make out the date on the nearest white one.

1956.

Stebbing must be very close.

She whimpered. Then she thought of God, who she really believed in. God wouldn't let Stebbing hurt her. She sort of reached out in her mind, to make sure God was there. In the windy night, He seemed very far away; but He *was* watching. Whimpering softly to herself, she walked on, trying not to look at the names on the tombstones, but not able to stop herself.

Stebbing was right by the path, third from the edge.

TO THE BELOVED MEMORY OF
BARRY STEBBING
BORN 11 MARCH 1944
DIED 22 JULY 1957
WITH GOD, WHICH IS MUCH BETTER

But Stebbing had nothing to say to her, here. Except, perhaps, a feeling it was all over, and his quarrel had never been with her. Really.

And then she was running, and the lights of home were in front of her, and Stebbing far behind.

She burst into the front hall like a hurricane. Daddy always kept the outside front door open, and a welcoming light glowing through the inner one, even in the middle of winter.

Daddy was standing by the hallstand, looking at her. Wearing his dark grey overcoat, and carrying a little bag like a doctor's. Instinctively, as the child of the vicarage, she knew he was going to somebody who was dying.

'Oh,' she said, 'I wanted to talk to you.' All breathless.

He smiled, but from far away; as God had. He always seemed far away, when he was going to somebody who was dying.

'You'll have to wait, Person, I'm afraid. But I expect I'll be home for tea. And all the evening. The Church Aid meeting's been cancelled.'

'Oh, *good*.' Toast made at the fire, and Daddy, and a long warm evening with the curtains drawn against the dark . . .

'I wonder,' he said vaguely, 'can you help? Is Millbrook Gardens the second or third turn off Windsor Road? I can never remember . . .'

'Second from the bottom.' Then, in a rush, 'Who's dying?'

He smiled, puzzled. They never talked about such things. 'Just an old man called Barnett . . . heart giving out. But his wife says he's very troubled . . . wants to talk about something he did years ago that's on his mind. I'd better be off, Rebeccah. See you soon.' He went out. She heard his footsteps fading down the path.

She clutched the hallstand desperately, her eyes screwed tight shut, so she wouldn't see her face in the mirror.

'Come home soon, Daddy,' she prayed. 'Come home soon.'

Fairy tales

Fairy tales, which had been passed down orally through families, were first collected and published in France in the seventeenth century. The stories that we know well today – *Cinderella, Sleeping Beauty, Little Red Riding Hood* and *Puss in Boots* – are derived from *Histoires ou contes du temps passé* ('Tales of long ago') collected by Charles Perrault in 1697. Even after being collected and published, fairy tales continued to evolve – sometimes appearing as a horror story, or instead as a cautionary tale; sometimes clearly for adults, or instead edited for children. This section has three stories. It begins with *Hansel and Gretel*, which you should read first to remind yourself of the basic plots of other fairy tales that you know.

Sweet Shop – Marc Alexander
This clever modern short story is based on a traditional fairy tale. As you read it, note the ways in which the author has transformed the text to make it relevant and topical for a modern teenage audience.

The Werewolf – Angela Carter
Carter is a modern English writer, famous for dark disturbing stories that use material from fairy tales and folk myths. As you read *The Werewolf*, note how she has based her tale on a traditional fairy story and the ways in which the old tale has been modernised.

Hansel and Gretel
The Brothers Grimm

At the edge of a great forest, there once lived a poor woodcutter with his wife and two children. The little boy was called Hansel, and the girl's name was Gretel. There was never much to eat in the house, and once, during a famine, the woodcutter could no longer put bread on the table. At night, he lay in bed worrying, tossing and turning in his distress. He sighed and said to his wife: 'What will become of us? How can we provide for our poor children when we don't even have enough for ourselves?'

'Listen to me,' answered the wife. 'Tomorrow at the break of day we'll take the children out into the darkest part of the woods. We'll make a fire for them and give them each a piece of bread. Then we'll go about our work and leave them alone. They'll never find their way home, and then we'll be rid of them.'

'No,' her husband replied. 'I won't do it. How could I have the heart to leave the children all alone in the woods when wild beasts would surely come and tear them to pieces?'

'You fool,' she said. 'Then all four of us will starve to death. You might as well start planing the boards for our coffins.'

She didn't give him a moment's peace until he consented. 'But still, I feel sorry for the poor children,' he said.

The two children hadn't been able to sleep either, because they were so hungry, and they heard everything that their stepmother had said to their father. Gretel wept bitter tears and said to Hansel. 'Well, now we're lost.'

'Be quiet, Gretel,' said Hansel, 'and stop worrying. I'll figure out something.'

As soon as the old folks had fallen asleep, he got up, put on his little jacket, opened the lower half of the door, and slipped out. The moon was shining brightly, and the white pebbles in front of the house were glittering like silver coins. Hansel stooped down and put as many as would fit into his jacket pocket. Then he went back and said to Gretel: 'Don't worry, dear little sister. Sleep peacefully. God will not forsake us.' And he went back to bed.

At daybreak, just before the sun had risen, the wife came and woke the two children. 'Get up, you lazybones, we're going to go into the forest to get some wood.'

The wife gave each child a little piece of bread and said: 'Here's something for lunch. But don't eat it before then, because you're not getting anything else.'

Gretel put the bread under her apron because Hansel had the pebbles in his pocket. Then they all set out together on the path into the forest. After a little while, Hansel stopped to look back at the house. He did that again and again. His father said: 'Hansel, why are you always stopping and staring? Watch out, and don't forget what your legs are for.'

'Oh, Father,' said Hansel. 'I'm looking at my white kitten, which is sitting up on the roof trying to bid me farewell.'

The woman said: 'You fool, that's not your kitten. Those are the rays of the sun, shining on the chimney.'

But Hansel had not been looking at the kitten. He had been taking the shiny pebbles from his pocket and dropping them on the ground.

When they arrived in the middle of the forest, the father said: 'Go gather some wood, children. I'll build a fire so that you won't get cold.'

Hansel and Gretel gathered brushwood until they had a little pile of it. The brushwood was lit, and when the flames were high enough, the woman said: 'Now lie down by the fire, children, and get some rest. We're going into the forest to chop some wood. When we're done, we'll come back to get you.'

Hansel and Gretel sat by the fire. At noon they ate their little pieces of bread. Since they could hear the sounds of an axe, they were sure that their father was close by. But it wasn't an axe that they heard, it was a branch that their father had fastened to a dead tree, and the wind was banging it back and forth. They were sitting there for such a long time that finally their eyes closed from fatigue, and they fell fast asleep. When they awoke, it was pitch dark. Gretel began to cry and said: 'How will we ever get out of the woods!'

Hansel comforted her: 'Just wait until the moon has risen. Then we will find the way back.'

And when the full moon had risen, Hansel took his sister by the hand and followed the pebbles, which were shimmering like newly minted coins and pointed the way for them. They walked all night long and arrived at their father's house just as day was breaking. They knocked at the door, and when the woman opened the door and saw that it was Hansel and Gretel, she said: 'You wicked children! Why did you sleep so long in the woods? We thought you weren't ever going to come back.'

But the father was overjoyed, because he had been upset at how he had abandoned them in the forest.

Not long after that, every square inch of the country was stricken by famine, and one night the children could hear what the mother was saying to their father when they were in bed: 'We've eaten everything up again. All that's left is half a loaf of bread, then the jig's up. The children have to go. This time we'll take them deeper into the forest so that they won't find the way out. Otherwise there's no hope for us.'

Her husband's heart was heavy, and he thought: 'It would be better if you shared the last crumb of bread with your children.' But the woman would not listen to anything that he said. She fussed and berated him. In for a penny, in for a pound, and since he had given in the first time, he had to give in a second time.

The children were still awake and had heard the conversation. When their parents had fallen asleep, Hansel got up and wanted to go out to pick up some pebbles as he had the last time, but the woman had locked the door, and Hansel couldn't get out. But he comforted his sister and said: 'Don't cry, Gretel. Just sleep peacefully. The Lord will protect us.'

Early the next morning the woman came and woke the children up. They each got a little piece of bread, this time even smaller than last time. On the way into the woods, Hansel crushed the bread in his pocket and would often stop to scatter crumbs on the ground.

'Hansel, why are you stopping and staring?' asked the father. 'Keep going!'

'I'm looking at my little dove, the one sitting on the roof and trying to bid me farewell,' Hansel replied.

'Fool,' said the woman. 'That isn't your little dove. Those are the rays of the morning sun shining up on the chimney.'

After a while, Hansel had scattered all the crumbs on the path.

The woman took the children even deeper into the woods, where they had never been before in their lives. Once again a large fire was built, and the mother said: 'Don't move from there, children. If you get tired, you can sleep for a while. We're going to go into the forest to chop wood. In the evening, when we're done, we'll come to get you.'

At noon Gretel shared her bread with Hansel, who had scattered bits of his piece on the path. Then they fell asleep. The evening went by, but no one came to get the poor children. They awoke when it was pitch dark, and Hansel comforted his sister by saying: 'Just wait, Gretel, until the moon rises. Then we will be able to see the crumbs of bread I scattered. They will point the way home for us.'

When the moon rose, they set off, but they couldn't find the crumbs because the many thousands of birds flying about in the forest and over the fields had eaten them. Hansel said to Gretel: 'We'll find the way back,' but they didn't find it. They walked all night long and then another day from early in the morning until late at night. But they couldn't find their way out of the woods, and they got more and more hungry, for they had nothing to eat but a few berries they found on the ground. When they became so tired that their legs would no longer carry them, they lay down under a tree and fell asleep.

It was now the third morning after they had left their father's house. They started walking again, but they just got deeper and deeper into the woods. If they didn't get help soon, they were sure to perish. At noon they saw a beautiful bird, white as snow, perched on a branch. It was singing so beautifully that they stopped to listen. When it had finished its song, it flapped its wings and flew on ahead of them. They followed it until they came to a little house, and the bird perched on its roof. As they approached the house, they realised that it was built of bread and had a roof made of cake and transparent windows of sugar.

'Let's see what it tastes like,' said Hansel. 'May the Lord bless our meal. I'll try a piece of the roof, Gretel, and you can try the window. That's sure to taste sweet.' Hansel reached up and broke off a small piece of the roof to see what it tasted like. Gretel went over to the windowpane and nibbled on it. Suddenly a gentle voice called from inside:

'Nibble, nibble, is it a mouse?
Who's that nibbling at my house?'

The children replied:

'The wind so mild,
The heavenly child.'

and they continued eating, without getting distracted. Hansel, who liked the taste of the roof, tore off a big piece of it, and Gretel knocked out an entire windowpane and sat down on the ground to savor it. Suddenly the door opened, and a woman as old as the hills, leaning on a crutch, hobbled out. Hansel and Gretel were so terrified that they dropped everything in their hands. The old woman said, with her head shaking: 'Well, dear children, how in the world did you get here? Come right inside and stay with me. You will not meet with any harm here.'

She took them by the hand and led them into her little house. They were served a wonderful meal of milk and pancakes with sugar, apples, and nuts. Later, two beautiful little beds were made up with white sheets. Hansel and Gretel lay down in them and felt as if they were in heaven.

The old woman had only pretended to be so friendly. She was really a wicked witch, who lay in wait for children. She had built the little house of bread just to lure them inside. As soon as a child was in her power, she killed it, cooked it, and ate it. That was a real feast day for her. Witches have red eyes and can't see very far, but they have a keen sense of smell, like animals, and they can always tell when a human being is around. When Hansel and Gretel got near her, she laughed fiendishly and sneered: 'They're mine! This time they won't get away from me!' Early in the morning, before the children were awake, she got out of bed and looked at the two of them resting so sweetly, with their full red cheeks. She muttered to herself: 'They will make a tasty morsel.'

Then she grabbed Hansel with her scrawny hand, took him to a small shed, and closed the barred door on him. He could cry as loud as he wanted, it did him no good. Then she went over to Gretel, shook her until she woke up, and cried out: 'Get up, lazy bones, fetch some water and cook your brother something good. He's staying outside in a shed, waiting to be fattened up. When he's put on enough weight, I'll eat him.'

Gretel began to cry bitter tears, but it did no good. She had to do what the wicked witch demanded. The finest food was cooked for poor Hansel, and Gretel got nothing but crab shells. Every morning the old woman would slink over to the little shed and cry out: 'Hansel, hold out your finger so that I can tell if you're plump enough.'

Hansel would stick a little bone out, and the old woman, who had poor eyesight, thought that it was Hansel's finger and wondered why he wasn't putting on weight. When four weeks had passed and Hansel was still as scrawny as ever, she lost her patience and decided not to wait any longer. 'Hey there, Gretel,' she called out to the girl, 'go get some water and be quick about it. I don't care whether Hansel's plump or scrawny. He's going to be slaughtered tomorrow, and then I'll cook him.'

'Oh,' the poor little sister wailed, and how the tears flowed down her cheeks! 'Dear God, help us,' she cried out. 'If only the wild animals in the forest had eaten us, at least then we would have died together.'

'Spare me your blubbering!' the old woman said. 'Nothing can help you now.'

Early in the morning Gretel had to go fill the kettle with water and light the fire. 'First we'll do some baking,' the old woman said. 'I've already heated up the oven and kneaded the dough.'

She pushed poor Gretel over to the oven, from which flames were leaping. 'Crawl in,' said the witch, 'and see if it's hot enough to slide the bread in.'

The witch was planning to shut the door as soon as Gretel got into the oven. Then she was going to bake her and eat her up too. But Gretel saw what was on her mind and said: 'I don't know how to get in there. How can I manage it?'

'Silly goose,' said the old woman. 'The opening is big enough. Just look. Even I can get in,' and she scrambled over to it and stuck her head in the oven. Gretel gave her a big push that sent her sprawling. Then she shut the iron door and bolted it. Phew! the witch began screeching dreadfully. But Gretel ran away and the godless witch burned miserably to death.

Gretel ran straight to Hansel, opened the little shed and cried out: 'Hansel, we're saved! The old witch is dead.'

Hansel hopped out as soon as the door opened, like a bird leaving its cage. How thrilled they were: they hugged and kissed, and jumped up and down for joy! Since there was nothing more to fear, they went right into the witch's house. In every corner there were chests filled with pearls and jewels. 'These are even better than pebbles,' said Hansel and put what he could into his pockets.

Gretel said, 'I'll take something home too,' and she filled up her little apron.

'Let's get going now,' said Hansel 'We need to get out of this witch's forest.'

When they had walked for a few hours, they reached a large body of water. 'We can't get across,' said Hansel. 'There's not a bridge in sight.'

'There aren't any ships around,' Gretel said, 'but here comes a white duck. It will help us cross, if I ask it.' She called out:

> 'Help us, help us, little duck
> Hansel and Gretel are out of luck.
> There's no bridge, not far or wide,
> Help us, give us both a ride.'

The duck came paddling over. Hansel got on it and told his sister to sit down next to him. 'No,' said Gretel, 'that would be too heavy a load for the little duck. It can take us over one at a time.'

That's just what the good little creature did. When they were safely on the other side and had walked for some time, the woods became more and more familiar. Finally they could see their father's house from afar. They began running, and then they raced into their father's house, throwing their arms around him. The man had not had a happy hour since the day that he had abandoned the children in the forest. His wife had died. Gretel emptied her apron and the pearls and jewels rolled all over the floor. Hansel reached into his pockets and pulled out one handful of jewels after another. Their worries were over, and they lived together in perfect happiness.

My fairy tale is done. See the mouse run. Whoever catches it can make a great big fur hat out of it.

Sweet Shop
Marc Alexander

To the girl it seemed an age since the day her troubles had begun – Black Monday she called it – but in fact it was only the week before. On that afternoon she sat in Eng. Lit. class fiddling with her hair ribbon, which she always did when she was bored, while Mr South rambled on about fairy tales, of all things.

'There's a lot more to traditional fairy stories than you ever imagined when your teacher read "Jack and the Beanstalk" to you in the Infants,' he said, his specs flashing as they always did when he tried to get the class interested in his subject. 'What people thought of as magic in them was really glimpses of the future . . .'

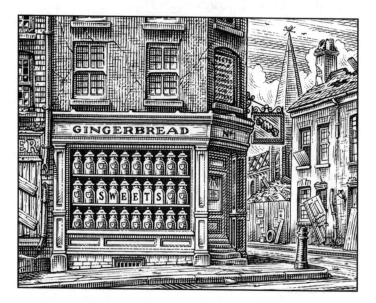

'Do you believe in all that, sir?' asked Hughie Cooper in a voice so respectful that some of the class could not help giggling.

'Oh yes, he does!' someone called out as they do in the panto.

'Oh no, he don't!' the class chorused, and this went on for a while. When it was quiet again Mr South said, 'Think of what I was saying – in the story of Snow White there was a magic mirror. What would that be today?'

'The telly, sir,' the class answered.

'And Seven-League Boots?'

Everyone shouted something different, and in the end Mr South agreed with those who said motor cars.

'And the Magic Carpet?'

'Please, sir,' said Hughie Cooper, 'isn't the Magic Carpet in *The Arabian Nights*, sir? Not in fairy tales, sir?'

Mr South pretended not to hear, and beamed when Betty Reynolds said, 'Concorde, sir?'

'What about "Puss in Boots", sir?' a boy asked from the back.

'That's a moggy in a chemist's shop,' said Hughie and there was a gale of laughter.

Mr South was getting angry but the buzzer saved the situation. It was home time and laughs were over for the day.

'Now think about fairy stories,' he shouted over the banging of desk tops. 'Next lesson you will write me an essay on fairy-tale things in modern life . . .'

In the playground the girl met her brother – being a year older than her he was in another class – and they walked home together. She told him about Mr South and his soppy fairy tales and he told her how someone had worked out a new video game in computer studies, and before long they were in their street which ran down to the canal.

'Hey, there's Dad's bike against the fence,' the boy said. 'Wonder why he's home?'

Even as he spoke the girl felt scared – she just knew that something was wrong, and as soon as they went inside she found out what it was. Their father was sitting at the kitchen table with a funny-not-ha-ha look on his face and a mug of tea in front of him.

'Your dad's been made redundant!' shouted Dora, their father's second wife. They could not bring themselves to call her 'mother'.

'Twenty-five years I've been at Holroyd's,' he said slowly. 'And even if I say so myself I was their best joiner in the hand-made furniture shop – and now I've been chucked out like an old boot. Seems there's no call for hand-made furniture any more, so the whole shop's being closed. They'll carry on making mass-produced rubbish – probably with robots! – but they don't need craftsmen any more. And in my day it took a five years' apprenticeship to learn the skills . . .'

'Pity you hadn't learned something more useful,' Dora said with her special sniff.

'Like what?' her husband demanded.

'Like being a clerk with the Council or a traffic warden – you don't hear of them being made redundant.'

'But I'm a joiner. Whatever ability God gave me is in my hands.'

Dora sniffed again and dabbed her eyes with the tea towel.

'Don't take on, love,' he said. 'I'll get something else.'

'You've no chance,' she replied angrily. 'Half the factories in this town are closed, so who do you think would want you at your age!'

'You can't blame me for the recession! I did think I might find some sympathy in my own home.'

'So it's sympathy you want! But what about me? Did you think about me when you let them sack you? How am I going to manage, answer me that – with those two not bringing in a penny and eating their heads off? . . . It's about time they made their own way in the world.'

'Dora, they're only school kids.'

'They cost as much as adults to keep. With you on the Unemployment I don't know what will happen.'

Their father stood up and said in a shaky voice, 'Well, I'll be off down the Job Centre.' And he walked out.

The children exchanged a look and went outside but their father was already striding quickly down the long street.

'We'd better not go after him,' the girl said. 'He'll want to be alone for a bit.'

'Why the hell did he have to marry again?' demanded her brother.

'I suppose he was lonely.'

'He's got all the company he needs now. She could have laid off him on a day like this.'

Suddenly the girl laughed, a bitter, unsteady laugh. 'Now I know what old South was on about with his talk of fairy tales in the present day,' she said. 'There *are* still such things as witches!'

The boy looked bewildered so she said, 'Forget it – let's go down to the canal.'

When she was a little girl the canal bank had been her favourite place. In those days working boats tied up by the factories which backed on to the canal, but now a lot of them were empty and the boats did not come any more. The water was stagnant and people threw rubbish into it, but it was still peaceful. As the two children strolled along the old towpath they saw a silent angler with a fishing rod hoping to land a tiddler which had survived the pollution.

'As soon as I can I'm going away,' said the boy. Then he added, 'You can come with me, if you like.'

'Thanks.'

'I'm sick of it all – Dora's nagging, and the endless rows. We used to have such a good time. Seems like ages ago now.'

His sister took his hand but could think of nothing to say.

The canal ran through the town but as it was hidden away behind buildings most people had forgotten about it, which made it a secret way for the children to wander until they found they were in a part of the town which was strange to them.

'This must be the Old Town where the Council was going to build those new blocks of flats,' said the boy. 'Let's go and see what it's like.'

They went up a narrow passage between two warehouses and found themselves in a street where most of the houses had been knocked down. This had been done to make way for tower blocks but the Council had run out of money and the place looked like an old battlefield. Here and there a few houses, some lonely shops and a boarded-up church survived among the rubble. At the end of the street a building stood by itself and as the children drew nearer they gave whistles of surprise – it was a sweet shop. Its paint was bright, its glass shone in the sunlight, and it had a sign on which GINGERBREAD was painted in large golden letters.

They went up to the window and there was another surprise – it was crammed with the biggest assortment of sweets they had ever seen. The display was not made up of Mars bars and suchlike but old-fashioned lollies in big glass jars, sweets that their mother – their real mother – told them she used to get when she was a girl, and which had to be weighed and put in little white paper bags.

'It can't do much business here,' said the boy. 'But look at those jelly babies . . .'

'There's a jar of aniseed balls . . .'

'Gob stoppers . . .'

'Chocolate fish . . .'

'If you're so interested, why not come inside,' said a soft voice, and they saw a plump white-haired old lady smiling at them from the door. The only odd thing about her was her spectacles, which magnified her eyes to twice their normal size, but the children soon got used to her appearance.

Inside the shop she gave them different sweets to try until the boy, feeling he should spend some money, bought a quarter of Pontefract cakes.

'Look, I have some gingerbread men,' said the old lady. 'Do you know the story of the Gingerbread Man?'

'My mum told me when I was small, and I cried at the way the Gingerbread Man kept losing pieces of himself as he ran away,' the girl said. 'It seemed so sad.'

'But not for those who were eating him,' chuckled the old lady. She was pleased to have someone to talk to because, as she told them, she had lost most of her customers when the houses were demolished but she loved her shop and did not want to leave it. They stayed chatting with her until it was twilight outside, and they had forgotten what had happened at home.

'Come back to Gingerbread any time,' she said as they left. 'My name is Hazel – the kiddies used to call me Aunt Hazel. You can if you like.'

When they got back to the towpath the girl found that the old lady had slipped a big bar of fruit-and-nut into her pocket.

'What a nice old dear,' she said as she shared it with her brother.

'Her shop reminds me of a picture I once saw in a storybook,' he said. 'I didn't think there were any shops like that left.'

'It's a find. Perhaps I will come back and see her.'

'You're just out for free chocolate,' he teased.

Next morning the two children did not wait to have breakfast but hurried out. They were sick of the quarrelling that had flared up the night before, when Dora had accused them of always plotting against her because she had the bad luck to be their stepmother. It was something that had not occurred to her until their father had been made redundant.

When they reached the corner the boy said, 'I'm going to cut school today.'

The girl nodded.

'Let's go for a walk.'

'Poor Dad, all those years at Holroyd's . . . and Dora going on as though it's his fault.'

Without either of them discussing where they were going, they arrived at the cemetery. In front of the gravestone with their mother's name on it was a bunch of carnations, and they realised that it was not to the Job Centre that their father had gone the night before.

Later they found themselves wandering along the canal bank, a place where they were less likely to be reported for playing truant.

'I know,' said the boy suddenly. 'Let's go and see Aunt Hazel – you might get given another bar of chocolate.'

They arrived at the shop called Gingerbread and had just enough money to buy a quarter of old-fashioned cough candy.

'You're not at school?' said Aunt Hazel, staring at them with her magnified eyes.

'We gave ourselves a holiday,' the girl said, and she laughed.

'I'm glad. I was feeling lonely. Sometimes I don't open the shop in the mornings because no one comes – my only customers are kids from the council estate over there, and they come after school. But I'm glad I opened up today because you both look as though you have troubles.'

'We're all right,' said the boy quickly.

'Good, but as you are on holiday you can at least have a cup of tea with me.'

Having missed breakfast they were happy to follow her into her living-room which was just as quaint as the shop, and full of old-fashioned furniture which would have delighted their father. In front of an open fireplace dozed one of the biggest black cats they had ever seen, and there was a parrot in a big cage who chattered, 'Open the door – let me out.'

Aunt Hazel tapped the cage and said, 'Silly thing, you know Samkin would have your tailfeathers the moment you were outside.' But the parrot kept on saying 'Let me out' until she put a cloth over his cage and he thought it was night-time.

'Why do you have bars at the window?' the boy asked.

'Now that I have no neighbours I'm nervous of burglars,' Aunt Hazel replied. 'The bars make me feel safe – a burglar would need a blowtorch to get in.'

'But he might come through the door.'

'Look.' She put a key into a keyhole close to the doorway and steel bars shot across it. 'I can operate the bars from the shop too, in case anyone tries to get through to the house in the daytime, and at night I'm safe as a bank,' she said. 'It cost a lot to get them fitted but at my age you don't want to be worried each time the house creaks.'

'That's enough of me – tell me about yourselves while you have your tea,' she added as she went to a cupboard which was stocked with cakes and biscuits.

She seemed so kind – rather like a nice granny – that the children found themselves telling her about their father being made redundant, how they did not get on with their stepmother, and how they would like to leave home. It was a great relief to talk about their problems to a sympathetic grown-up.

'She makes a change from Dora,' the boy whispered as they left her at the shop door, waving goodbye and telling them to visit her again.

'She likes you,' the girl said. 'All the time we were having tea and eating those gingerbread men she kept looking at you. Perhaps she wishes she'd been married and had a son.'

'I'm going to run away – to London,' he said suddenly.

The next few days were a nightmare for the girl. Her father looked ill and did not know what to do with himself except to go to the Job Centre each morning. Her brother was moody and silent and stayed away from school, and she was terrified that he would leave home without telling her.

One morning his stepmother found out that he was missing classes and there was an angry scene.

'You won't get any qualifications and you'll end up on the Unemployment like your father!' she yelled.

'Haven't we got enough trouble without you adding to it?' his father asked him.

The boy ran out of the house, slamming the door so hard that Dora's collection of china draught-horses rattled on the sideboard.

His sister left soon afterwards, and it seemed that the furious voices coming from the house followed her. She wanted to find her brother quickly because she knew how his mind worked, and she guessed that when he stormed out he had made his mind up never to return. First she went to the cemetery, expecting that he would be paying a last visit before he hitch-hiked away from the grimy old town, but she found no one there. Then she was certain where he had gone, and in a few minutes she reached the canal.

The only living things she saw were two swans which, for some reason, made her think about Mr South and his fairy tales . . . something to do with the Swan Princess, she supposed. How she wished she lived in a fairy-tale land where all you had to worry about was dragons and ogres and wicked dwarfs – much better than real problems!

She was out of breath by the time she found herself in the demolished street where the sweet shop stood alone at the far end.

'Aunt Hazel,' she called when she went inside but there was no answer. It was the squawk of the parrot which made her open the door behind the counter and step into the living-room with its pretty furniture and barred windows.

To her horror she saw her brother in front of the open cupboard and he was *stealing*. 'How could you?' She gasped. 'And from such a nice old lady?'

'I'm not taking much,' he answered. 'Not money or anything – just some biscuits and scones to keep me going until I reach London.'

'It's still stealing,' she said. 'You should've asked.'

'I don't want anybody to talk me out of going,' he answered in a sulky voice, 'and that goes for you, too.'

She was about to give him an angry reply when there was a grating sound and the steel rods slid across the doorway behind her. Then Aunt Hazel appeared in the shop, her huge eyes peering at them through the bars as though they were animals in a zoo cage.

'Well, well, the chicks have returned to the gingerbread house,' she chuckled. 'Welcome back, Hansel and Gretel.'

The Werewolf
Angela Carter

It is a northern country; they have cold weather, they have cold hearts.

Cold; tempest; wild beasts in the forest. It is a hard life. Their houses are built of logs, dark and smoky within. There will be a crude icon of the virgin behind a guttering candle, the leg of a pig hung up to cure, a string of drying mushrooms. A bed, a stool, a table. Harsh, brief, poor lives.

To these upland woodsmen, the Devil is as real as you or I. More so; they have not seen us nor even know that we exist, but the Devil they glimpse often in the graveyards, those bleak and touching townships of the dead where the graves are marked with portraits of the deceased in the naïf style and there are no flowers to put in front of them, no flowers grow there, so they put out small, votive offerings, little loaves, sometimes a cake that the bears come lumbering from the margins of the forest to snatch away. At midnight, especially on Walpurgisnacht, the Devil holds picnics in the graveyards and invites the witches; then they dig up fresh corpses, and eat them. Anyone will tell you that.

Wreaths of garlic on the doors keep out the vampires. A blue-eyed child born feet first on the night of St John's Eve will have second sight. When they discover a witch – some old woman whose cheeses ripen when her neighbours' do not, another old woman whose black cat, oh, sinister! *follows her about all the time*, they strip the crone, search for her marks, for the supernumerary nipple her familiar sucks. They soon find it. Then they stone her to death.

* * *

Winter and cold weather.

Go and visit grandmother, who has been sick. Take her the oatcakes I've baked for her on the hearthstone and a little pot of butter.

The good child does as her mother bids – five miles' trudge through the forest; do not leave the path because of the bears, the wild boar, the starving wolves. Here, take your father's hunting knife; you know how to use it.

The child had a scabby coat of sheepskin to keep out the cold, she knew the forest too well to fear it but she must always be on her guard. When she heard that freezing howl of a wolf, she dropped her gifts, seized her knife and turned on the beast.

It was a huge one, with red eyes and running, grizzled chops; any but a mountaineer's child would have died of fright at the sight of it. It went for her throat, as wolves do, but she made a great swipe at it with her father's knife and slashed off its right forepaw.

The wolf let out a gulp, almost a sob, when it saw what had happened to it; wolves are less brave than they seem. It went lolloping off disconsolately between the trees as well as it could on three legs, leaving a trail of blood behind it. The child wiped the blade of her knife clean on her apron, wrapped up the wolf's paw in the cloth in which her mother had packed the oatcakes and went on towards her grandmother's house. Soon it came on to snow so thickly that the path and any footsteps, track or spoor that might have been upon it were obscured.

She found her grandmother was so sick she had taken to her bed and fallen into a fretful sleep, moaning and shaking so that the child guessed she had a fever. She felt the forehead, it burned. She shook out the cloth from her basket, to use it to make the old woman a cold compress, and the wolf's paw fell to the floor.

But it was no longer a wolf's paw. It was a hand, chopped off at the wrist, a hand toughened with work and freckled with old age. There was a wedding ring on the third finger and a wart on the index finger. By the wart, she knew it for her grandmother's hand.

She pulled back the sheet but the old woman woke up at that, and began to struggle, squawking and shrieking like a thing possessed. But the child was strong, and armed with her father's hunting knife; she managed to hold her grandmother down long enough to see the cause of her fever. There was a bloody stump where her right hand should have been, festering already.

The child crossed herself and cried out so loud the neighbours heard her and came rushing in. They knew the wart on the hand at once for a witch's nipple; they drove the old woman, in her shift as she was, out into the snow with sticks, beating her old carcass as far as the edge of the forest, and pelted her with stones until she fell down dead.

Now the child lived in her grandmother's house; she prospered.

Crime fiction

This section on crime fiction features two stories with differing styles. Although both contain the necessary elements of the genre, the two tales were written some years apart – one is narrated in the first person, the other in the third person. Does this have any effect on the level of suspense for you as the reader?

The Adventure of the Sussex Vampire – Sir Arthur Conan Doyle

Sir Arthur Conan Doyle (1859–1930) created one of the most famous fictional detectives, Sherlock Holmes. He based this character on a man called John Bell, one of his university professors who had a very logical and deductive mind. Notice how the character of Holmes is the intelligent and perceptive detective, traditional of this genre. The story is narrated by Dr Watson, Holmes's assistant, and we are guided through Holmes's deductions by this character who has to think his way through the mystery, just like us.

Lamb to the Slaughter – Roald Dahl

Many of you will know Roald Dahl for his children's stories such as *James and the Giant Peach* and *Matilda*. He is also famous as a writer for adults, and published many thrilling and sometimes disturbing short stories. This modern crime story is interesting to compare and contrast with more traditional examples of the detective genre such as the Sherlock Holmes stories. Here Roald Dahl describes a modern setting and situation, and gives us a rather different perspective on the modern detective or police officer.

The Adventure of the Sussex Vampire
Sir Arthur Conan Doyle

Holmes had read carefully a note which the last post had brought him. Then, with the dry chuckle which was his nearest approach to a laugh, he tossed it over to me.

'For a mixture of the modern and the medieval, of the practical and of the wildly fanciful, I think this is surely the limit,' said he. 'What do you make of it, Watson?'

I read as follows:

46 OLD JEWRY,
Nov. 19th

Re Vampires

SIR,

Our client, Mr Robert Ferguson, of Ferguson and Muirhead, tea brokers, of Mincing Lane, has made some inquiry from us in a communication of even date concerning vampires. As our firm specialises entirely upon the assessment of machinery the matter hardly comes without our purview, and we have therefore recommended Mr Ferguson to call upon you and lay the matter before you. We have not forgotten your successful action in the case of Matilda Briggs.

We are, Sir, Faithfully yours,

MORRISON, MORRISON AND DODD
per E.J.C.

'Matilda Briggs was not the name of a young woman, Watson,' said Holmes in a reminiscent voice. 'It was a ship which is associated with the giant rat of Sumatra, a story for which the world is not yet prepared. But what do we know about vampires? Does it come within our purview either? Anything is better than stagnation, but really we seem to have been switched on to a Grimm's fairytale. Make a long arm, Watson, and see what V has to say.'

I leaned back and took down the great index volume to which he referred. Holmes balanced it on his knee and his eyes moved slowly and lovingly over the record of old cases, mixed with the accumulated information of a lifetime.

'Voyage of the *Gloria Scott*,' he read. 'That was a bad business. I have some recollection that you made a record of it, Watson, though I was unable to congratulate you upon the result. Victor Lynch, forger. Venomous lizard or gila. Remarkable case, that! Vittoria, the circus belle. Vanderbilt and the Yeggman. Vipers, Vogir, the Hammersmith wonder. Hullo! Hullo! Good old index. You can't beat it. Listen to this, Watson. Vampirism in Hungary. And again, Vampires in Transylvania.' He turned over the pages with eagerness, but after a short intent perusal he threw down the great book with a snarl of disappointment.

'Rubbish, Watson, rubbish! What have we to do with walking corpses who can only be held in their grave by stakes driven through their hearts? It's pure lunacy.'

'But surely,' said I, 'the vampire was not necessarily a dead man? A living person might have the habit. I have read, for example, of the old sucking the blood of the young in order to retain their youth.'

'You are right, Watson. It mentions the legend in one of these references. But are we to give serious attention to such things? This Agency stands flatfooted upon the ground, and there it must remain. The world is big enough for us. No ghosts need apply. I fear that we cannot take Mr Robert Ferguson very seriously. Possibly this note may be from him, and may throw some light upon what is worrying him.'

He took up a second letter which had lain unnoticed upon the table whilst he had been absorbed with the first. This he began to read with a smile of amusement upon his face which gradually faded away into an expression of intense interest and concentration. When he had finished he sat for some little time lost in thought with the letter dangling from his fingers. Finally, with a start, he aroused himself from his reverie.

'Cheeseman's, Lamberley. Where is Lamberley, Watson?'

'It is in Sussex, south of Horsham.'

'Not very far, eh? And Cheeseman's?'

'I know that country, Holmes. It is full of old houses which are named after the men who built them centuries ago. You get Odley's and Harvey's and Carriton's – the folk are forgotten but their names live in their houses.'

'Precisely,' said Holmes coldly. It was one of the peculiarities of his proud, self-contained nature that, though he docketed any fresh information very quickly and accurately in his brain, he seldom made any acknowledgement to the giver. 'I rather fancy we shall know a good deal more about Cheeseman's, Lamberley, before we are through. The letter is, as I had hoped, from Robert Ferguson. By the way, he claims acquaintance with you.'

'With me!'

'You had better read it.'

He handed the letter across. It was headed with the address quoted.

DEAR MR HOLMES, [it said]

I have been recommended to you by my lawyers, but indeed the matter is so extraordinarily delicate that it is most difficult to discuss. It concerns a friend for whom I am acting. This gentleman married some five years ago a Peruvian lady, the daughter of a Peruvian merchant, whom he had met in connection with the importation of nitrates. The lady was very beautiful, but the fact of her foreign birth and of her alien religion always caused a separation of interests and of feelings between husband and wife, so that after a time his love may have cooled towards her and he may have come to regard their union as a mistake. He felt there were sides of her character which he could never explore or understand. This was the more painful as she was as loving a wife as a man could have – to all appearance absolutely devoted.

Now for the point which I will make more plain when we meet. Indeed, this note is merely to give you a general idea of the situation and to ascertain whether you would care to interest yourself in the matter. The lady began to show some curious traits quite alien to her ordinarily sweet and gentle disposition. The gentleman had been married twice and he had one son by the first wife. This boy was now fifteen, a very charming and affectionate youth, though unhappily injured through an accident in childhood. Twice the wife was caught in the act of assaulting this poor lad in the most unprovoked way. Once she struck him with a stick and left a great weal on his arm.

This was a small matter, however, compared with the conduct to her own child, a dear boy just under one year of age. On one occasion about a month ago this child had been left by its nurse for a few minutes. A loud cry from the baby, as of pain, called the nurse back. As she ran into the room she saw her employer, the lady, leaning over the baby and apparently biting his neck. There was a small wound in the neck, from which a stream of blood had escaped. The nurse was so horrified that she wished to call the husband, but the lady implored her not to do so, and actually gave her five pounds as a price for her silence. No explanation was ever given, and for the moment the matter was passed over.

It left, however, a terrible impression upon the nurse's mind, and from that time she began to watch her mistress closely, and to keep a closer guard upon the baby, whom she tenderly loved. It seemed to her that even as she watched the mother, so the mother watched her, and that every time she was compelled to leave the baby alone the mother was waiting to get at it. Day and night the nurse covered the child, and day and night the silent, watchful mother seemed to be lying in wait as a wolf waits for a lamb. It must read most incredible to you, and yet I beg you to take it seriously, for a child's life and a man's sanity may depend upon it.

At last there came one dreadful day when the facts could no longer be concealed from the husband. The nurse's nerve had given way; she could stand the strain no longer, and she made a clean breast of it all to the man. To him it seemed as wild a tale as it may now seem to you. He knew his wife to be a loving wife, and, save for the assaults upon her stepson, a loving mother. Why, then, should she wound her own dear little baby? He told the nurse that she was dreaming, that her suspicions were those of a lunatic, and that such libels upon her mistress were not to be tolerated. Whilst they were talking, a sudden cry of pain was heard. Nurse and master rushed together to the nursery. Imagine his feelings, Mr Holmes, as he saw his wife rise from a kneeling position beside the cot, and saw blood upon the child's exposed neck and upon the sheet. With a cry of horror, he turned his wife's face to the light and saw blood all round her lips. It was she – she beyond all question – who had drunk the poor baby's blood.

So the matter stands. She is now confined to her room. There has been no explanation. The husband is half demented. He knows, and I know, little of Vampirism beyond the name. We had thought it was some wild tale of foreign parts. And yet here in the very heart of English Sussex – well, all this can be discussed with you in the morning. Will you see me? Will you use your great powers in aiding a distracted man? If so, kindly wire to Ferguson, Cheeseman's, Lamberley, and I will be at your rooms by ten o'clock.

Yours faithfully,

ROBERT FERGUSON

PS. - I believe your friend Watson played Rugby for Blackheath when I was three-quarter for Richmond. It is the only personal introduction which I can give.

'Of course I remember him,' said I, as I laid down the letter. 'Big Bob Ferguson, the finest three-quarter Richmond ever had. He was always a good-natured chap. It's like him to be so concerned over a friend's case.'

Holmes looked at me thoughtfully and shook his head.

'I never get your limits, Watson,' said he. 'There are unexplored possibilities about you. Take a wire down, like a good fellow. "Will examine your case with pleasure."'

'Your case!'

'We must not let him think that this Agency is a home for the weak-minded. Of course it is his case. Send him that wire and let the matter rest till morning.'

Promptly at ten o'clock next morning Ferguson strode into our room. I had remembered him as a long, slab-sided man with loose limbs and a fine turn of speed, which had carried him round many an opposing back. There is surely nothing in life more painful than to meet the wreck of a fine athlete whom one has known in his prime. His great frame had fallen in, his flaxen hair was scanty, and his shoulders were bowed. I fear that I roused corresponding emotions in him.

'Hullo, Watson,' said he, and his voice was still deep and hearty. 'You don't look quite the man you did when I threw you over the ropes into the crowd at the Old Deer Park. I expect I have changed a bit also. But it's this last day or two that has aged me. I see by your telegram, Mr Holmes, that it is no use my pretending to be anyone's deputy.'

'It is simpler to deal direct,' said Holmes.

'Of course it is. But you can imagine how difficult it is when you are speaking of the one woman you are bound to protect and help. What can I do? How am I to go to the police with such a story? And yet the kiddies have got to be protected. Is it madness, Mr Holmes? Is it something in the blood? Have you any similar case in your experience? For God's sake, give me some advice, for I am at my wits' end.'

'Very naturally, Mr Ferguson. Now sit here and pull yourself together and give me a few clear answers. I can assure you that I am far from being at my wits' end, and that I am confident we shall find some solution. First of all, tell me what steps you have taken. Is your wife still near the children?'

'We had a dreadful scene. She is a most loving woman, Mr Holmes. If ever a woman loved a man with all her heart and soul, she loves me. She was cut to the heart that I should have discovered this horrible, this incredible, secret. She would not even speak. She gave no answer to my reproaches, save to gaze at me with a wild, despairing look in her eyes. Then she rushed to her room and locked herself in. Since then she has refused to see me. She has a maid who was with her before her marriage, Dolores by name – a friend rather than a servant. She takes her food to her.'

'Then the child is in no immediate danger?'

'Mrs Mason, the nurse, has sworn that she will not leave it night or day. I can absolutely trust her. I am more uneasy about poor little Jack, for, as I told you in my note, he has twice been assaulted by her.'

'But never wounded?'

'No; she struck him savagely. It is the more terrible as he is a poor little inoffensive cripple.' Ferguson's gaunt features softened as he spoke of his boy. 'You would think that the dear lad's condition would soften anyone's heart. A fall in childhood and a twisted spine, Mr Holmes. But the dearest, most loving heart within.'

Holmes had picked up the letter of yesterday and was reading it over. 'What other inmates are there in your house, Mr Ferguson?'

'Two servants who have not been long with us. One stable-hand, Michael, who sleeps in the house. My wife, myself, my boy Jack, baby, Dolores and Mrs Mason. That is all.'

'I gather that you did not know your wife well at the time of your marriage?'

'I had only known her a few weeks.'

'How long had this maid Dolores been with her?'

'Some years.'

'Then your wife's character would really be better known by Dolores than by you?'

'Yes, you may say so.'

Holmes made a note.

'I fancy,' said he, 'that I may be of more use at Lamberley than here. It is eminently a case for personal investigation. If the lady remains in her room, our presence could not annoy or inconvenience her. Of course, we would stay at the inn.'

Ferguson gave a gesture of relief.

'It is what I hoped, Mr Holmes. There is an excellent train at two from Victoria, if you could come.'

'Of course we could come. There is a lull at present. I can give you my undivided energies. Watson, of course, comes with us. But there are one or two points upon which I wish to be very sure before I start. This unhappy lady as I understand it, has appeared to assault both the children, her own baby, and your little son?'

'That is so.'

'But the results take different forms, do they not? She has beaten your son.'

'Once with a stick and once very savagely with her hands.'

'Did she give no explanation why she struck him?'

'None, save that she hated him. Again and again she said so.'

'Well, that is not unknown among stepmothers. A posthumous jealousy, we will say. Is the lady jealous by nature?'

'Yes, she is very jealous – jealous with all the strength of her fiery tropical love.'

'But the boy – he is fifteen, I understand, and probably very developed in mind, since his body has been circumscribed in action. Did he give you no explanation of these assaults?'

'No; he declared there was no reason.'

'Were they good friends at other times?'

'No: there was never any love between them.'

'Yet you say he is affectionate?'

'Never in the world could there be so devoted a son. My life is his life. He is absorbed in what I say or do.'

Once again Holmes made a note. For some time he sat lost in thought.

'No doubt you and the boy were great comrades before this second marriage. You were thrown very close together, were you not?'

'Very much so.'

'And the boy, having so affectionate a nature, was devoted, no doubt, to the memory of his mother?'

'Most devoted.'

'He would certainly seem to be a most interesting lad. There is one other point about these assaults. Were the strange attacks upon the baby and the assaults upon your son at the same period?'

'In her first case it was so. It was as if some frenzy had seized her, and she had vented her rage upon both. In the second case it was only Jack who suffered. Mrs Mason had no complaint to make about the baby.'

'That certainly complicates matters.'

'I don't quite follow you, Mr Holmes.'

'Possibly not. One forms provisional theories and waits for time or fuller knowledge to explode them. A bad habit, Mr Ferguson; but human nature is weak. I fear that your old friend here has given an exaggerated view of my scientific methods. However, I will only say at the present stage that your problem does not appear to me to be insoluble, and that you may expect to find us at Victoria at two o'clock.'

It was evening of a dull, foggy November day when, having left our bags at The Chequers, Lamberley, we drove through the Sussex clay of a long winding lane, and finally reached the isolated and ancient farmhouse in which Ferguson dwelt. It was a large, straggling building, very old in the centre, very new at the wings, with towering Tudor chimneys and a lichen-spotted, high-pitched roof of Horsham slabs. The doorsteps were worn into curves, and the ancient tiles which lined the porch were marked with the rebus of a cheese and a man, after the original builder. Within, the ceilings were corrugated with heavy oaken beams, and the uneven floors sagged into sharp curves. An odour of age and decay pervaded the whole crumbling building.

There was one very large central room, into which Ferguson led us. Here, in a huge old-fashioned fireplace with an iron screen behind it dated 1670, there blazed and spluttered a splendid log fire.

The room, as I gazed round, was a most singular mixture of dates and of places. The half-panelled walls may well have belonged to the original yeoman farmer of the seventeenth century. They were ornamented, however, on the lower part by a line of well-chosen modern water-colours; while above, where yellow plaster took the place of oak, there was hung a fine collection of South American utensils and weapons, which had been brought, no doubt, by the Peruvian lady upstairs. Holmes rose, with that quick curiosity which sprang from his eager mind, and examined them with some care. He returned with his eyes full of thought.

'Hullo!' he cried. 'Hullo!'

A spaniel had lain in a basket in the corner. It came slowly forward towards its master, walking with difficulty. Its hind-legs moved irregularly and its tail was on the ground. It licked Ferguson's hand.

'What is it, Mr Holmes?'

'The dog. What's the matter with it?'

'That's what puzzled the vet. A sort of paralysis. Spinal meningitis, he thought. But it is passing. He'll be all right soon – won't you, Carlo?'

A shiver of assent passed through the drooping tail. The dog's mournful eyes passed from one of us to the other. He knew that we were discussing his case.

'Did it come on suddenly?'

'In a single night.'

'How long ago?'

'It may have been four months ago.'

'Very remarkable. Very suggestive.'

'What do you see in it, Mr Holmes?'

'A confirmation of what I had already thought.'

'For God's sake, what do you think, Mr Holmes? It may be a mere intellectual puzzle to you, but it is life and death to me! My wife a would-be murderer – my child in constant danger! Don't play with me, Mr Holmes. It is too terribly serious.'

The big rugby three-quarter was trembling all over. Holmes put his hand soothingly upon his arm.

'I fear that there is pain for you, Mr Ferguson, whatever the solution may be,' said he. 'I would spare you all I can.

I cannot say more for the instant, but before I leave this house I hope I may have something definite.'

'Please God you may! If you will excuse me, gentlemen, I will go up to my wife's room and see if there has been any change.'

He was away some minutes, during which Holmes resumed his examination of the curiosities upon the wall. When our host returned it was clear from his downcast face that he had made no progress. He brought with him a tall, slim girl.

'The tea is ready, Dolores,' said Ferguson. 'See that your mistress has everything she can wish.'

'She verra ill,' cried the girl, looking with indignant eyes at her master. 'She no ask for food. She verra ill. She need doctor. I frightened stay alone with her without doctor.'

Ferguson looked at me with a question in his eyes.

'I should be so glad if I could be of use.'

'Would your mistress see Dr Watson?'

'I take him. I no ask leave. She needs doctor.'

'Then I'll come with you at once.'

I followed the girl, who was quivering with strong emotion, up the staircase and down an ancient corridor. At the end was an iron-clamped and massive door.

It struck me as I looked at it that if Ferguson tried to force his way to his wife he would find it no easy matter. The girl drew a key from her pocket, and the heavy oaken planks creaked upon their old hinges. I passed in and she swiftly followed, fastening the door behind her.

On the bed a woman was lying who was clearly in a high fever. She was only half conscious, but as I entered she raised a pair of frightened but beautiful eyes and glared at me in apprehension. Seeing a stranger, she appeared to be relieved, and sank back with a sigh upon the pillow. I stepped up to her with a few reassuring words, and she lay still while I took her pulse and temperature. Both were high, and yet my impression was the condition was rather that of mental and nervous excitement than of any actual seizure.

'She lie like that one day, two day. I 'fraid she die,' said the girl.

The woman turned her flushed and handsome face towards me.

'Where is my husband?'

'He is below, and would wish to see you.'

'I will not see him. I will not see him.' Then she seemed to wander off into delirium. 'A fiend! A fiend! Oh, what shall I do with this devil?'

'Can I help you in any way?'

'No. No one can help. It is finished. All is destroyed. Do what I will, all is destroyed.'

The woman must have some strange delusion. I could not see honest Bob Ferguson in the character of fiend or devil.

'Madame,' I said, 'your husband loves you dearly. He is deeply grieved at this happening.'

Again she turned on me those glorious eyes.

'He loves me. Yes. But do I not love him? Do I not love him even to sacrifice myself rather than break his dear heart. That is how I love him. And yet he could think of me – he could speak to me so.'

'He is full of grief, but he cannot understand.'

'No, he cannot understand. But he should trust.'

'Will you not see him?' I suggested.

'No, no; I cannot forget those terrible words nor the look upon his face. I will not see him. Go now. You can do nothing for me. Tell him only one thing. I want my child. I have a right to my child. That is the only message I can send him.' She turned her face to the wall and would say no more.

I returned to the room downstairs, where Ferguson and Holmes still sat by the fire. Ferguson listened moodily to my account of the interview.

'How can I send her the child?' he said. 'How do I know what strange impulse might come upon her? How can I ever forget how she rose from beside it with its blood on her lips?' He shuddered at the recollection. 'The child is safe with Mrs Mason, and there he must remain.'

A smart maid, the only modern thing which we had seen in the house, had brought in some tea. As she was serving it the door opened and a youth entered the room. He was a remarkable lad, pale-faced and fair-haired, with excitable light blue eyes which blazed into a sudden flame of emotion and joy as they rested upon his father. He rushed forward and threw his arms round his neck with the abandon of a loving girl.

'Oh, Daddy,' he cried. 'I did not know that you were due yet. I should have been here to meet you. Oh, I am so glad to see you!'

Ferguson gently disengaged himself from the embrace with some little show of embarrassment.

'Dear old chap,' said he, patting the flaxen head with a very tender hand. 'I came early because my friends, Mr Holmes and Dr Watson, have been persuaded to come down and spend an evening with us.'

'Is that Mr Holmes, the detective?'

'Yes.'

The youth looked at us with a very penetrating and, as it seemed to me, unfriendly gaze.

'What about your other child, Mr Ferguson?' asked Holmes. 'Might we make the acquaintance of the baby?'

'Ask Mrs Mason to bring baby down,' said Ferguson. The boy went off with a curious, shambling gait which told my surgical eyes that he was suffering from a weak spine. Presently he returned, and behind him came a tall, gaunt woman bearing in her arms a very beautiful child, dark-eyed, golden-haired, a wonderful mixture of the Saxon and the Latin. Ferguson was evidently devoted to it, for he took it into his arms and fondled it most tenderly.

'Fancy anyone having the heart to hurt him,' he muttered, as he glanced down at the small, angry red pucker upon the cherub throat.

It was at this moment that I chanced to glance at Holmes, and saw a most singular intentness in his expression. His face was as set as if it had been carved out of old ivory, and his eyes, which had glanced for a moment at father and child, were now fixed with eager curiosity upon something at the other side of the room. Following his gaze I could only guess that he was looking out through the window at the melancholy, dripping garden. It is true that a shutter had half closed outside and obstructed the view, but none the less it was certainly at the window that Holmes was fixing his concentrated attention. Then he smiled, and his eyes came back to the baby. On its chubby neck there was this small puckered mark. Without speaking, Holmes examined it with care. Finally he shook one of the dimpled fists which waved in front of him.

'Goodbye, little man. You have made a strange start in life. Nurse, I should wish to have a word with you in private.'

He took her aside and spoke earnestly for a few minutes. I only heard the last words, which were: 'Your anxiety will soon, I hope, be set at rest.' The woman, who seemed to be a sour, silent kind of creature, withdrew with the child.

'What is Mrs Mason like?' asked Holmes.

'Not very prepossessing externally, as you can see, but a heart of gold, and devoted to the child.'

'Do you like her, Jack?' Holmes turned suddenly upon the boy. His expressive mobile face shadowed over, and he shook his head.

'Jacky has very strong likes and dislikes,' said Ferguson, putting his arm round the boy. 'Luckily I am one of his likes.'

The boy cooed and nestled his head upon his father's breast. Ferguson gently disengaged him.

'Run away, little Jacky,' said he, and he watched his son with loving eyes until he disappeared. 'Now, Mr Holmes,' he continued, when the boy was gone. 'I really feel that I have brought you on a fool's errand, for what can you possibly do, save give your sympathy? It must be an exceedingly delicate and complex affair from your point of view.'

'It is certainly delicate,' said my friend, with an amused smile, 'but I have not been struck up to now with its complexity. It has been a case for intellectual deduction, but when this original intellectual deduction is confirmed point by point by quite a number of independent incidents, then the subjective becomes objective and we can say confidently that we have reached our goal. I had, in fact, reached it before we left Baker Street, and the rest has merely been observation and confirmation.'

Ferguson put his big hand to his furrowed forehead.

'For Heaven's sake, Holmes,' he said hoarsely, 'if you can see the truth in this matter, do not keep me in suspense. How do I stand? What shall I do? I care nothing as to how you have found your facts so long as you have really got them.'

'Certainly I owe you an explanation, and you shall have it. But you will permit me to handle the matter in my own way? Is the lady capable of seeing us, Watson?'

'She is ill, but she is quite rational.'

'Very good. It is only in her presence that we can clear the matter up. Let us go up to her.'

'She will not see me,' cried Ferguson.

'Oh, yes, she will,' said Holmes. He scribbled a few lines upon a sheet of paper. 'You at least have the *entrée*, Watson. Will you have the goodness to give the lady this note?'

I ascended again and handed the note to Dolores, who cautiously opened the door. A minute later I heard a cry from within, a cry in which joy and surprise seemed to be blended. Dolores looked out.

'She will see them. She will leesten,' said she.

At my summons Ferguson and Holmes came up. As we entered the room Ferguson took a step or two towards his wife, who had raised herself in the bed, but she held out her hand to repulse him. He sank into an armchair, while Holmes seated himself beside him, after bowing to the lady, who looked at him with wide-eyed amazement.

'I think we can dispense with Dolores,' said Holmes.

'Oh, very well, madame, if you would rather she stayed I can see no objection. Now, Mr Ferguson, I am a busy man with many calls, and my methods have to be short and direct. The swiftest surgery is the least painful. Let me first say what will ease your mind. Your wife is a very good, a very loving, and a very ill-used woman.'

Ferguson sat up with a cry of joy.

'Prove that, Mr Holmes, and I am your debtor for ever.'

'I will do so, but in doing so I must wound you deeply in another direction.'

'I care nothing so long as you clear my wife. Everything on earth is insignificant compared to that.'

'Let me tell you, then, the train of reasoning which passed through my mind in Baker Street. The idea of a vampire was to me absurd. Such things do not happen in criminal practice in England. And yet your observation was precise. You had seen the lady rise from beside the child's cot with the blood upon her lips.'

'I did.'

'Did it not occur to you that a bleeding wound may be sucked for some other purpose than to draw the blood from it? Was there not a Queen in English history who sucked such a wound to draw poison from it?'

'Poison!'

'A South American household. My instinct felt the presence of those weapons upon the wall before my eyes ever saw them. It might have been other poison, but that was what occurred to me. When I saw that little empty quiver beside the small bird-bow, it was just what I expected to see. If the child were pricked with one of those arrows dipped in curare or some other devilish drug, it would mean death if the venom were not sucked out.

'And the dog! If one were to use such a poison, would one not try it first in order to see that it had not lost its power? I did not foresee the dog, but at least I understood him and he fitted into my reconstruction.

'Now do you understand? Your wife feared such an attack. She saw it made and saved the child's life, and yet she shrank from telling you all the truth, for she knew how you loved the boy and feared lest it break your heart.'

'Jacky!'

'I watched him as you fondled the child just now. His face was clearly reflected in the glass of the window where the shutter formed a background. I saw such jealousy, such cruel hatred, as I have seldom seen in a human face.'

'My Jacky!'

'You have to face it, Mr Ferguson. It is the more painful because it is a distorted love, a maniacal exaggerated love for you, and possibly for his dead mother, which has prompted his action. His very soul is consumed with hatred for this splendid child, whose health and beauty are a contrast to his own weakness.'

'Good God! It is incredible!'

'Have I spoken the truth, madame?'

The lady was sobbing, with her face buried in the pillows. Now she turned to her husband.

'How could I tell you, Bob? I felt the blow it would be to you. It was better that I should wait and that it should come from some other lips than mine. When this gentleman, who seems to have powers of magic, wrote that he knew all, I was glad.'

'I think a year at sea would be my prescription for Master Jacky,' said Holmes, rising from his chair. 'Only one thing is still clouded, madame. We can quite understand your attacks upon Master Jacky. There is a limit to a mother's patience. But how did you dare to leave the child these last two days?'

'I had told Mrs Mason. She knew.'

'Exactly. So I imagined.'

Ferguson was standing by the bed, choking, his hands outstretched and quivering.

'This, I fancy, is the time for our exit, Watson,' said Holmes in a whisper. 'If you will take one elbow of the too faithful Dolores, I will take the other. There, now,' he added, as he closed the door behind him. 'I think we may leave them to settle the rest among themselves.'

I have only one further note in this case. It is the letter which Holmes wrote in final answer to that with which the narrative begins. It ran thus:

BAKER STREET,
Nov. 21st

Re Vampires

SIR,

Referring to your letter of the 19th, I beg to state that I have looked into the inquiry of your client, Mr Robert Ferguson, of Ferguson and Muirhead, tea brokers, of Mincing Lane, and that the matter has been brought to a satisfactory conclusion. With thanks for you recommendation.

I am, Sir,

Faithfully yours,

SHERLOCK HOLMES

Lamb to the Slaughter
Roald Dahl

The room was warm and clean, the curtains drawn, the two table lamps alight – hers and the one by the empty chair opposite. On the sideboard behind her, two tall glasses, soda water, whisky. Fresh ice cubes in the Thermos bucket.

Mary Maloney was waiting for her husband to come home from work.

Now and again she would glance up at the clock, but without anxiety, merely to please herself with the thought that each minute gone by made it nearer the time when he would come. There was a slow smiling air about her, and about everything she did. The drop of the head as she bent over her sewing was curiously tranquil. Her skin – for this was her sixth month with child – had acquired a wonderful translucent quality, the mouth was soft, and the eyes, with their new placid look, seemed larger, darker than before.

When the clock said ten minutes to five, she began to listen, and a few moments later, punctually as always, she heard the tyres on the gravel outside, and the car door slamming, the footsteps passing the window, the key turning in the lock. She laid aside her sewing, stood up, and went forward to kiss him as he came in.

'Hullo, darling,' she said.

'Hullo,' he answered.

She took his coat and hung it in the closet. Then she walked over and made the drinks, a strongish one for him, a weak one for herself; and soon she was back again in her chair with the sewing, and he in the other, opposite, holding the tall glass with both his hands, rocking it so the ice cubes tinkled against the side.

For her, this was always a blissful time of day. She knew he didn't want to speak much until the first drink was finished, and she, on her side, was content to sit quietly, enjoying his company after the long hours alone in the house. She loved to luxuriate in the presence of this man, and to feel – almost as a sunbather feels the sun – that warm male glow that came out of him to her when they were alone together. She loved him for the way he sat loosely in a chair, for the way he came in a door, or moved slowly across the room with long strides. She loved the intent, far look in his eyes when they rested on her, the funny shape of the mouth, and especially the way he remained silent about his tiredness, sitting still with himself until the whisky had taken some of it away.

'Tired, darling?'

'Yes,' he said. 'I'm tired.' And as he spoke, he did an unusual thing. He lifted his glass and drained it in one swallow although there was still half of it, at least half of it, left. She wasn't really watching him but she knew what he had done because she heard the ice cubes falling back against the bottom of the empty glass when he lowered his arm. He paused a moment, leaning forward in the chair, then he got up and went slowly over to fetch himself another.

'I'll get it!' she cried, jumping up.

'Sit down,' he said.

When he came back, she noticed that the new drink was dark amber with the quantity of whisky in it.

'Darling, shall I get your slippers?'

'No.'

She watched him as he began to sip the dark yellow drink, and she could see little oily swirls in the liquid because it was so strong.

'I think it's a shame,' she said, 'that when a policeman gets to be as senior as you, they keep him walking about on his feet all day long.'

He didn't answer, so she bent her head again and went on with her sewing; but each time he lifted the drink to his lips, she heard the ice cubes clinking against the side of the glass.

'Darling,' she said. 'Would you like me to get you some cheese? I haven't made any supper because it's Thursday.'

'No,' he said.

'If you're too tired to eat out,' she went on, 'it's still not too late. There's plenty of meat and stuff in the freezer, and you can have it right here and not even move out of the chair.'

Her eyes waited on him for an answer, a smile, a little nod, but he made no sign.

'Anyway,' she went on, 'I'll get you some cheese and crackers first.'

'I don't want it,' he said.

She moved uneasily in her chair, the large eyes still watching his face. 'But you *must* have supper. I can easily do it here. I'd like to do it. We can have lamb chops. Or pork. Anything you want. Everything's in the freezer.'

'Forget it,' he said.

'But, darling, you *must* eat! I'll fix it anyway, and then you can have it or not, as you like.'

She stood up and placed her sewing on the table by the lamp.

'Sit down,' he said. 'Just for a minute, sit down.'

It wasn't till then that she began to get frightened.

'Go on,' he said. 'Sit down.'

She lowered herself back slowly into the chair, watching him all the time with those large, bewildered eyes. He had finished the second drink and was staring into the glass, frowning.

'Listen,' he said, 'I've got something to tell you.'

'What is it, darling? What's the matter?'

He had become absolutely motionless, and he kept his head down so that the light from the lamp beside him fell across the upper part of his face, leaving the chin and mouth in shadow. She noticed there was a little muscle moving near the corner of his left eye.

'This is going to be a bit of a shock to you, I'm afraid,' he said. 'But I've thought about it a good deal and I've decided the only thing to do is tell you right away. I hope you won't blame me too much.'

And he told her. It didn't take long, four or five minutes at most, and she sat very still through it all, watching him with a kind of dazed horror as he went further and further away from her with each word.

'So there it is,' he added. 'And I know it's kind of a bad time to be telling you, but there simply wasn't any other way. Of course I'll give you money and see you're looked after. But there needn't really be any fuss. I hope not anyway. It wouldn't be very good for my job.'

Her first instinct was not to believe any of it, to reject it all. It occurred to her that perhaps he hadn't even spoken, that she herself had imagined the whole thing. Maybe, if she went about her business and acted as though she hadn't been listening, then later, when she sort of woke up again, she might find none of it had ever happened.

'I'll get the supper,' she managed to whisper, and this time he didn't stop her.

When she walked across the room she couldn't feel her feet touching the floor. She couldn't feel anything at all – except a slight nausea and a desire to vomit. Everything was automatic now – down the stairs to the cellar, the light switch, the deep freeze, the hand inside the cabinet taking hold of the first object it met. She lifted it out, and looked at it. It was wrapped in paper, so she took off the paper and looked at it again.

A leg of lamb.

All right then, they would have lamb for supper. She carried it upstairs, holding the thin bone-end of it with both her hands, and as she went through the living-room, she saw him standing over by the window with his back to her, and she stopped.

'For God's sake,' he said, hearing her, but not turning round, 'Don't make supper for me. I'm going out.'

At that point, Mary Maloney simply walked up behind him and without any pause she swung the big frozen leg of lamb high in the air and brought it down as hard as she could on the back of his head.

She might just as well have hit him with a steel club.

She stepped back apace, waiting, and the funny thing was that he remained standing there for at least four or five seconds, gently swaying. Then he crashed to the carpet.

The violence of the crash, the noise, the small table overturning, helped bring her out of the shock. She came out slowly, feeling cold and surprised, and she stood for a while blinking at the body, still holding the ridiculous piece of meat tight with both hands.

All right, she told herself. So I've killed him.

It was extraordinary, now, how clear her mind became all of a sudden. She began thinking very fast. As the wife of a detective, she knew quite well what the penalty would be. That was fine. It made no difference to her. In fact, it would be a relief. On the other hand, what about the child? What were the laws about murderers with unborn children? Did they kill them both – mother and child? Or did they wait until the tenth month? What did they do?

Mary Maloney didn't know. And she certainly wasn't prepared to take a chance.

She carried the meat into the kitchen, placed it in a pan, turned the oven on high, and shoved it inside. Then she washed her hands and ran upstairs to the bedroom. She sat down before the mirror, tidied her hair, touched up her lips and face. She tried a smile. It came out rather peculiar. She tried again.

'Hullo Sam,' she said brightly, aloud.

The voice sounded peculiar too.

'I want some potatoes please, Sam. Yes, and I think a can of peas.'

That was better. Both the smile and the voice were coming out better now. She rehearsed it several times more. Then she ran downstairs, took her coat, went out the back door, down the garden, into the street.

It wasn't six o'clock yet and the lights were still on in the grocery shop.

'Hullo Sam,' she said brightly, smiling at the man behind the counter.

'Why, good evening, Mrs Maloney. How're *you*?'

'I want some potatoes please, Sam. Yes, and I think a can of peas.'

The man turned and reached up behind him on the shelf for the peas.

'Patrick's decided he's tired and doesn't want to eat out tonight,' she told him. 'We usually go out Thursdays, you know, and now he's caught me without any vegetables in the house.'

'Then how about meat, Mrs Maloney?'

'No, I've got meat, thanks. I got a nice leg of lamb, from the freezer.'

'Oh.'

'I don't much like cooking it frozen, Sam, but I'm taking a chance on it this time. You think it'll be all right?'

'Personally,' the grocer said, 'I don't believe it makes any difference. You want these Idaho potatoes?'

'Oh yes, that'll be fine. Two of those.'

'Anything else?' The grocer cocked his head on one side, looking at her pleasantly. 'How about afterwards? What you going to give him for afterwards?'

'Well – what would you suggest, Sam?'

The man glanced around his shop. 'How about a nice big slice of cheesecake? I know he likes that.'

'Perfect,' she said. 'He loves it.'

And when it was all wrapped and she had paid, she put on her brightest smile and said, 'Thank you, Sam. Good night.'

'Good night, Mrs Maloney. And thank *you*.'

And now, she told herself as she hurried back, all she was doing now, she was returning home to her husband and he was waiting for his supper; and she must cook it good, and make it as tasty as possible because the poor man was tired; and if, when she entered the house, she happened to find anything unusual, or tragic, or terrible, then naturally it would be a shock and she'd become frantic with grief and horror. Mind you, she wasn't *expecting* to find anything. She was just going home with the vegetables. Mrs Patrick Maloney going home with the vegetables on Thursday evening to cook supper for her husband.

That's the way, she told herself. Do everything right and natural. Keep things absolutely natural and there'll be no need for any acting at all.

Therefore, when she entered the kitchen by the back door, she was humming a little tune to herself and smiling.

'Patrick!' she called. 'How are you, darling?'

She put the parcel down on the table and went through into the living-room; and when she saw him lying there on the floor with his legs doubled up and one arm twisted back underneath his body, it really was rather a shock. All the old love and longing for him welled up inside her, and she ran over to him, knelt down beside him, and began to cry her heart out. It was easy. No acting was necessary.

A few minutes later she got up and went to the phone. She knew the number of the police station, and when the man at the other end answered, she cried to him, 'Quick! Come quick! Patrick's dead!'

'Who's speaking?'

'Mrs Maloney. Mrs Patrick Maloney.'

'You mean Patrick Maloney's dead?'

'I think so,' she sobbed. 'He's lying on the floor and I think he's dead.'

'Be right over,' the man said.

The car came very quickly, and when she opened the front door, two policemen walked in. She knew them both – she knew nearly all the men at the precinct – and she fell right into Jack Noonan's arms, weeping hysterically. He put her gently into a chair, then went over to join the other one, who was called O'Malley, kneeling by the body.

'Is he dead?' she cried.

'I'm afraid he is. What happened?'

Briefly, she told her story about going out to the grocer and coming back to find him on the floor. While she was talking, crying and talking, Noonan discovered a small patch of congealed blood on the dead man's head. He showed it to O'Malley who got up at once and hurried to the phone.

Soon, other men began to come into the house. First a doctor, then two detectives, one of whom she knew by name. Later, a police photographer arrived and took pictures, and a man who knew about fingerprints. There was a great deal of whispering and muttering beside the corpse, and the detectives kept asking her a lot of questions. But they always treated her kindly. She told her story again, this time right from the beginning, when Patrick had come in, and she was sewing, and he was tired, so tired he hadn't wanted to go out for supper. She told how she'd put the meat in the oven – 'it's there now, cooking' – and how she'd slipped out to the grocer for vegetables, and come back to find him lying on the floor.

'Which grocer?' one of the detectives asked.

She told him, and he turned and whispered something to the other detective who immediately went outside into the street.

In fifteen minutes he was back with a page of notes, and there was more whispering, and through her sobbing she heard a few of the whispered phrases – ' . . . acted quite normal . . . very cheerful . . . wanted to give him a good supper . . . peas . . . cheesecake . . . impossible that she . . .'

After a while, the photographer and the doctor departed and two other men came in and took the corpse away on a stretcher. Then the fingerprint man went away. The two detectives remained, and so did the two policemen. They were exceptionally nice to her, and Jack Noonan asked if she wouldn't rather go somewhere else, to her sister's house perhaps, or to his own wife who would take care of her and put her up for the night.

No, she said. She didn't feel she could move even a yard at the moment. Would they mind awfully if she stayed just where she was until she felt better? She didn't feel too good at the moment, she really didn't.

Then hadn't she better lie down on the bed? Jack Noonan asked.

No, she said, she'd like to stay right where she was, in this chair. A little later perhaps, when she felt better, she would move.

So they left her there while they went about their business, searching the house. Occasionally one of the detectives asked her another question. Sometimes Jack Noonan spoke to her gently as he passed by. Her husband, he told her, had been killed by a blow on the back of the head administered with a heavy blunt instrument, almost certainly a large piece of metal. They were looking for the weapon. The murderer may have taken it with him, but on the other hand he may've thrown it away or hidden it somewhere on the premises.

'It's the old story,' he said. 'Get the weapon, and you've got the man.'

Later, one of the detectives came up and sat beside her. Did she know, he asked, of anything in the house that could've been used as the weapon? Would she mind having a look around to see if anything was missing – a very big spanner, for example, or a heavy metal vase.

They didn't have any heavy metal vases, she said.

'Or a big spanner?'

She didn't think they had a big spanner. But there might be some things like that in the garage.

The search went on. She knew that there were other policemen in the garden all around the house. She could hear their footsteps on the gravel outside, and sometimes she saw the flash of a torch through a chink in the curtains. It began to get late, nearly nine she noticed by the clock on the mantel. The four men searching the rooms seemed to be growing weary, a trifle exasperated.

'Jack,' she said, 'the next time Sergeant Noonan went by. 'Would you mind giving me a drink?'

'Sure I'll give you a drink. You mean this whisky?'

'Yes, please. But just a small one. It might make me feel better.'

He handed her the glass.

'Why don't you have one yourself,' she said. 'You must be awfully tired. Please do. You've been very good to me.'

'Well,' he answered. 'It's not strictly allowed, but I might take just a drop to keep me going.'

One by one the others came in and were persuaded to take a little nip of whisky. They stood around rather awkwardly with the drinks in their hands, uncomfortable in her presence, trying to say consoling things to her. Sergeant Noonan wandered into the kitchen, came out quickly and said, 'Look, Mrs Maloney. You know that oven of yours is still on, and the meat still inside.'

'Oh *dear* me!' she cried. 'So it is!'

'I better turn it off for you, hadn't I?'

'Will you do that, Jack. Thank you so much.'

When the sergeant returned the second time, she looked at him with her large, dark, tearful eyes. 'Jack Noonan,' she said.

'Yes?'

'Would you do me a small favour – you and these others?'

'We can try, Mrs Maloney.'

'Well,' she said. 'Here you all are, and good friends of dear Patrick's too, and helping to catch the man who killed him. You must be terribly hungry by now because it's long past your supper time, and I know Patrick would never forgive me, God bless his soul, if I allowed you to remain in his house without offering you decent hospitality. Why don't you eat up that lamb that's in the oven? It'll be cooked just right by now.'

'Wouldn't dream of it,' Sergeant Noonan said.

'Please,' she begged. 'Please eat it. Personally I couldn't touch a thing, certainly not what's been in the house when he was here. But it's all right for you. It'd be a favour to me if you'd eat it up. Then you can go on with your work again afterwards.'

There was a good deal of hesitating among the four policemen, but they were clearly hungry, and in the end they were persuaded to go into the kitchen and help themselves. The woman stayed where she was, listening to them through the open door, and she could hear them speaking among themselves, their voices thick and sloppy because their mouths were full of meat.

'Have some more, Charlie?'

'No. Better not finish it.'

'She *wants* us to finish it. She said so. Be doing her a favour.'

'Okay then. Give me some more.'

'That's the hell of a big club the guy must've used to hit poor Patrick,' one of them was saying. 'The doc says his skull was smashed all to pieces just like from a sledge-hammer.'

'That's why it ought to be easy to find.'

'Exactly what I say.'

'Whoever done it, they're not going to be carrying a thing like that around with them longer than they need.'

One of them belched.

'Personally, I think it's right here on the premises.'

'Probably right under our very noses. What do you think, Jack?'

And in the other room, Mary Maloney began to giggle.

Love stories

This genre of literature includes many different styles of writing, for example: challenging literary works, Mills & Boon style romances, and more recent novels in the style of *Bridget Jones's Diary*. This section contains three stories that see the subject matter from different points of view. The stories also show that this genre doesn't always have the happy endings you might be looking for!

The Knight's Tale – Geoffrey Chaucer, retold by Geraldine McCaughrean

Chaucer is a famous figure in early English writing, best known for *The Canterbury Tales*, in which he gives a group of pilgrims tales to tell that fit their characters. This version of Chaucer's tale has been retold in modern English by Geraldine McCaughrean. As you read this romantic story try to think why the content of the tale is appropriate to a medieval knight.

Cinderella Girl – Vivien Alcock

This love story is written for young people and focuses on the need to be an individual rather than following the crowd in your choices in love. This is not always easy when other people such as parents and friends have strong opinions about who you should and should not like.

Gift – Susan Gates

Being 'in love' can often cloud our judgement of reality. The narrator of this story enjoys the romance of her ideas about a boy from her school. As you read this story look at how the first person narration is full of descriptive language that reflects her romantic state of mind.

The Knight's Tale:
Chivalry and Rivalry
Geoffrey Chaucer, retold
by Geraldine McCaughrean

Below the smoking walls of Thebes, two thousand men grappled, sword to sword and hand to hand. The battle between the forces of King Creon and the troops of Duke Theseus was long, fierce and bloody. And when it was over – when Creon's army had been put to flight – the ground was carpeted with fallen knights.

Athenian soldiers, searching the battlefield for their own wounded companions, found two young knights

lying side by side. But as they stepped across the two bodies, one stirred, groaned, and opened his eyes. 'Arcite! Cousin! Where are you?' he whispered.

His companion was not dead, either. Both were carried as prisoners to the tent of Duke Theseus. 'Take them to Athens, and lock them in the prison-tower of my palace,' said the Duke.

Despite the cold stones and hard floor of their tower-top prison, both Arcite and his cousin Palamon gradually recovered from their wounds. Their devoted friendship made the passing days, weeks and months bearable, though both grew dreadfully bored.

The narrow arrow slit, which let in the only sunlight they ever saw, overlooked the Duke's garden. Each day they would take it in turns to balance on a stool and gaze down at the flowers, and at the gardener pruning the rose-trees.

One day there was a new visitor to the garden. Palamon was balancing on the stool at the time, and his feet slipped and almost tipped it over. 'Oh Arcite!' he exclaimed. 'I never realized until this moment why I was born. Now I've seen her. She is the reason! Zeus! She can't be flesh and blood. She must be an angel!'

'Come down. It's my turn for the stool,' said Arcite, and he took Palamon's place.

Down in the garden, Duke Theseus' young sister-in-law, Emily, had come to gather flowers in a wicker basket. She sang as she picked them – and the flowers seemed to turn up their faces towards her, and to faint at the touch of her hand.

'Oh lady! I'll wear your favour until the day I die!' said Arcite breathlessly to himself.

Palamon pulled the stool away, and they both fell in a heap to the floor. 'What? Are you making fun of me, Arcite? It's serious! I'm in love with her!'

'You? You didn't even think she was human! It's I who love her.'

'You Judas! You cuckoo! Where are your vows of life-long friendship now? The first chance you get, you stab me in the back. You . . . you . . .'

'Viper! You thieving magpie!'

This undignified scene was interrupted by the gaoler bringing in their one frugal meal of the day. 'What's this, puppies?' he said, setting down the tray. 'Is this cell getting too small for the two of you? Well, I've got news for whichever one of you is Sir Arcite. Sir Arcite has a friend in Athens, it would appear. And this friend has spoken to Duke Theseus, and won your freedom. You can leave tomorrow.'

Arcite stared. Palamon got to his feet. 'Cousin!' he said. 'In all our lives, we have never been parted! Is there no message for *me*, gaoler? Has no one asked for *my* freedom?'

'No. You stay. And you, Sir Arcite, must be out of this land by sunset tomorrow. On pain of death are you forbidden to return.'

'Leave the country? Leave Athens? But I don't *want* to go!' protested Arcite. 'You go instead of me, Palamon. If I'm banished from Athens, I'll never see *her* again!'

Perhaps he saw, or perhaps he imagined a smile playing on Palamon's lips. Anyway, the two cousins, who all life long had been inseparable, barely spoke during that last night in the tower.

Next week, Palamon was still a captive, balancing all day on the stool to watch for Emily. Far away, his cousin sat in his own house, the windows and doors all shut as if it were a prison – for he was pining for Emily.

'Which do you think was better off?' mused the Knight, thoughtlessly interrupting his own story. 'Was it the man in prison or the man in exile?'

'Lord love you, have you no spark of wit?' demanded the lady I recognised from the night before by the enormous size of her hat. 'If the boy in exile had one half a brain he'd disguise himself and go back to Athens. If all he can do is sit around and mope, he doesn't *deserve* the woman!'

'Well, well,' said the Knight, rather taken aback by the strength of her feelings. 'That's just what happened.'

Arcite grew a beard, dressed as an Athenian, and took work as a servant in the very house where Emily lived. The thought of seeing her again quite outweighed the threat of death if he was discovered inside Athens.

Every day he saw her. Every day he took orders from her lips. Every day he was able to reach out and touch the chair where she had sat, the glass from which she had drunk. He thought he would be happy for ever.

He was happy for just a week. Then the questions began to creep into his mind. 'What good is this? How is this better than being in prison? How can a "servant" speak of love to the sister-in-law of Duke Theseus?' So he fell to brooding, to chewing his pillow at night, and cursing the hour he was born.

Just two hours after the gaoler forgot to lock the door of the prison tower, Palamon found himself free, creeping through the Athenian woods, his heart in his mouth, his life in the balance. 'Now's my only chance,' he thought. 'I'll find the lady Emily and ravish her away to my own country.'

A rustling of leaves sent him bolting like a rabbit into the bowl of a hollow tree. He squatted down low, despising his thumping heart, and despising his fate for bringing an honourable knight to such a pass.

The approaching footsteps halted beside the tree, and Palamon held his breath. Surely the Duke's men were not searching for him yet? Peeping through a knot-hole, he could see a man sitting dejectedly among the spreading roots, throwing pebbles at his own boots. 'What's the use?' he was muttering. 'I might just as well be rotting in prison with Palamon.'

'You asp! You wolf-in-sheep's clothing!' Palamon flung himself out of the tree and grabbed Arcite by his beard. 'What are you doing, sneaking back here to prowl round my Emily?'

'Don't you talk about my mistress and lady like that, you convict, you escaped prisoner!'

'I'm an honourable knight!' Palamon maintained, despite the hammer-blows Arcite was raining on his head. 'I love Emily far more than you do!'

'Heartsblood! Death's too good for you, you traitor to all things honourable!'

'Goat!'

'Skunk!'

'Rat!'

As they pranced, grunting through the trees, their arms locked fast round one another, a wolfhound came barking round their legs excitedly. There was another – and another – and another – until the clearing was awash with dogs. Into the mêlée burst a hunting party on horseback, and at its head Duke Theseus himself.

'Part those men and bring them here! One of them is Emily's serving-man. The other looks like one of Creon's men!'

'He is! He's an escaped convict!' Arcite shouted.

'And he's Arcite – banished on pain of death!' called Palamon. 'You see, cousin? I can play as dirty as you!'

Theseus laughed in disbelief. 'Is this the devoted twosome we took prisoner at Thebes? Bosom friends never to be parted? In the name of all that's friendly, what's this quarrel about?'

Arcite and Palamon wiped their muddy faces, and rubbed their bruised eyes. Then both together they said: 'HER!'

Emily had come riding into the clearing on a white mare. She wore a blue mantle, and even the hounds fell back whimpering at the sight of her.

Arcite sprang to one stirrup, Palamon to the other. 'Lady, your eye has scorched me like a burning-glass!'

'Emily! Your name is a millstone crushing my heart!'

'Sweetheart, if I were to live two hundred . . .'

'Enough!' roared Theseus. 'What is this competition of compliments? If you're going to compete, at least do it the man's way! Tomorrow I'm holding a joust. Both your lives are forfeit, but I shall spare the man who remains alive when the joust ends. Prepare yourselves – for tomorrow you fight in the lists!'

Not until sundown, when they were billetted in separate tents on the field of combat, did Palamon and Arcite stop quarrelling. Outside Arcite's tent, an armourer was sharpening a sword with a stone. It grated and screeched. A chill went through the knight, but he called to mind Emily's radiant face, and went happily to sleep. Outside Palamon's tent, a squire was sharpening his master's lance with a knife. The shavings fell on to the canopy and made shadows like a swarm of spiders. A chill went through Palamon, but he thought of Emily, and how pleased she would be by his chivalrous heroism, and he went to sleep contented.

The joust was a circus of colour. Knights caparisoned in mail, heraldic surcoats, and plumes fit for birds of paradise were brazed by the blaring of trumpets whose scarlet oriflammes were embroidered with silvery beasts. Blade by blade, the grass was turfed out in divots by the flying hoofs of horses. The pavilions flapped like Chinese kites. By midday, the ladies tripping back and forth to their seats had scarlet hems where their gowns had swept the field.

In the hottest part of the day, Arcite and Palamon found themselves at opposite ends of the jousting fence. Palamon's lance weighed heavy in the crook of his arm after so many months in prison. The squires blew a shrill fanfare. The horses rattled the bits between their teeth and pranced towards one another.

On the first pass, both lances missed their mark, and the two cousins passed shoulder to shoulder, grimacing into one another's face.

On the second pass, Palamon saw the point of Arcite's lance bearing squarely for his chest. He flung himself forward along his horse's neck, dropping his own lance. But the oncoming lance-tip tore through the back of his tunic, caught in his belt, and lifted him out of the saddle, pitching him to the ground. Arcite's lance was dragged from his grip, but he turned at the head of the lists and came galloping back down the field, swinging his mace.

Its iron spikes bruised the air with each whistling circle the mace-head made on its chain stalk. Palamon, his head uncovered, fell to his knees, but he knew he could not escape the swinging iron. In the grass, his hands brushed the lance that had dragged him from his horse. His fingers closed round its haft, and he was lifting it to protect himself, when Arcite, stretching from his saddle to strike the mortal blow, rode straight on to its point.

His face cleared of all expression. His horse rode from under him, and he stood for a moment with the lance planted in his chest. The mace dropped from his hand, and he spread his fingers across the red of his surcoat. 'Cousin,' he said, then fell dead on his back, the lance rising like a mast out of his hull.

Palamon took off his gauntlets and crawled across the grass to Arcite's side. 'Friend,' he said, touching his cousin's cheek. 'What have we done?'

Then the crowds were upon him, praising, congratulating. Duke Theseus was there, and Emily too, though Palamon could not recognise her at first among the other women. They were all quite pretty . . .

Theseus began: 'Arcite, my boy . . .'

'Palamon. I'm Palamon.'

'Oh. Well, Palamon, my boy, let this be an end to all quarrelling. Your rival has died a glorious death in the name of chivalry. And you have fought bravely, too. Take Emily's hand: and forget every unhappiness. The wedding shall be tomorrow!'

Hanging back in the shadow of her brother-in-law, Emily said: 'Urgh, do I have to? His hair's awfully thin already, and I don't like his mouth.' She had a voice like the teeth of a comb clicking.

'Nonsense, Emily. He's a very chivalrous knight – even if he is a foreigner. Emily – Arcite: my blessing on you both!'

'Palamon. I'm Palamon,' said the chivalrous knight, while at his feet Arcite raised no argument, no argument whatsoever.

The Knight stopped speaking. The woman in the enormous hat (who I learned was a widow all the way from Bath) had been leaning out of her saddle to catch the Knight's words. She was rather deaf, I think. She continued leaning towards him, waiting for more. 'Well?' she demanded in a huge, West Country voice. 'Were they happy?'

The Knight shook himself. 'Yes, oh yes. They both lived happily ever after. Palamon woke to each day happier than the day before.' The Widow smiled and sat back into her saddle with a thump.

'I don't know if he would – under the circumstances,' I said.

'Under *these* circumstances,' said the Knight, waving a hand towards the listening pilgrims, 'we had to have a happy ending. Now who's next?'

'All the same,' said a pebble-headed Reeve snarlingly, 'it wasn't a whole heap of laughs, your story.'

The Knight freely admitted it. 'I'm afraid I couldn't think of a *funny* story, offhand.'

'Well I can,' said the Reeve. We seemed to be about to hear his story, whether we liked it or not.

Cinderella Girl
Vivien Alcock

Bella Jones didn't like Meg Hunter one little bit. She was too rough, too noisy and too grubby.

'It's not only the way she crashes about, knocking things over,' she said. 'It's everything about her. She always looks such a fright. That great bush of hair, I bet she never combs it. And her face is often *dirty*. As for her clothes! She came to school yesterday with those horrible green trousers of hers done up with safety pins, did you notice? She just doesn't care what she looks like. She's an utter mess.'

It was true. Edward had to admit it. Yet there was something he liked about Meg, a sort of warm glow, a friendliness. She laughed a lot. The smaller kids loved her.

Meg was young for her age, that was the trouble, a big untidy girl with shaggy brown hair, like an overgrown puppy. She still climbed the trees on the common and rolled down the steep grass bank as he had done when he was a kid. He even saw her playing football with the boys from their old primary school, and had been tempted for a moment to join in. But the ground was wet and muddy, and he was wearing his new trousers. Also his mother was with him.

His mother liked people to look nice. 'It only takes a little effort to look clean and tidy,' she was fond of telling Edward, 'and it makes all the difference to what people think of you. Always remember that, Edward.' He knew she didn't approve of Meg. She never said so outright, but he could tell. Her plucked eyebrows always rose when she saw her, and she'd shake her head, as if to say, 'Well, really!'

'Isn't that Meg Hunter over there, playing football with those boys?' she'd asked. 'Covered in mud, poor girl. Just look at her! It's odd because her mother is really very nice, you know. And the two older girls are always beautifully dressed. You'd never take them for the same family. I wonder Mrs Hunter lets Meg go around looking like that.'

'She's Meg's stepmother,' Edward told her.

'It's not always easy being a stepmother,' his mother said. 'I imagine Meg can be quite a handful.'

A Cinderella girl, Edward thought. Poor Meg, nobody cares what she looks like. Perhaps her stepmother grudges every penny she has to spend on her, and won't buy her new clothes or even a hairbrush, so that she has to use safety pins when her zips break and comb her hair with her fingers.

'She's in your class, isn't she?' his mother asked.

'Yes.'

'Is she clever?'

'I don't know,' Edward said. 'I've never noticed.'

His mother laughed. 'I don't suppose you have,' she said. 'She's not the sort of girl boys look at.'

His mother didn't know everything, however. Edward did look at Meg, quite often. He wasn't certain why. She was plump and her clothes never seemed to fit her and she had big feet. On Sundays, however, when they met by chance in the park, they'd stay together, talking or watching their local team play football. He always looked forward to seeing her.

But it was Bella he really wanted to date. Pretty, popular Bella whom a lot of boys claimed would let you kiss her in the cinema or in the bushes behind the cycle shed. He had never kissed a girl, not properly, and was beginning to feel left out. Of course they might be only boasting.

'Have you ever kissed a girl?' he asked his best friend Michael, who was tall and skinny and clever, and could be trusted not to betray him.

'Of course I have! Millions of times. Can't get away from them,' Michael told him. 'They swarm over me every Christmas. Mum's only got to put up a bit of mistletoe and I have to hide to avoid being trampled on.'

'No, seriously, have you?'

'My lips are sealed,' Michael said grandly. 'I'm not one to kiss and tell.'

'I'm not asking for names. Just a straight answer, yes or no.'

'No. What about you?'

'No,' Edward admitted, 'but don't tell anybody.'

Michael laughed. 'Don't sound so sad. We're still young. Far too young, my mum would say. Do you want to kiss just any girl, or one in particular?'

'I want to kiss Bella Jones.'

'Oh, her! I might've guessed. You always want to do what other people do,' Michael said. He was not one of Bella's admirers. 'Well, why don't you?'

He made it sound easy. Full of hope, Edward had asked Bella to come to see a film with him.

'No, I don't think so,' she said.

'Why not?' he asked. 'I thought you liked me.'

'Whatever gave you that idea?' she said.

'Oh come on! There's a good film on at the Odeon. *Alligator Angel*. I'll treat you. What about tomorrow?'

She shook her head. 'Not tomorrow.'

'Wednesday?'

'Sorry. Can't manage Wednesday.'

'What about Thursday, then?'

'I dunno. I might. I'll think about it,' she said.

On Thursday morning, he came to school early, in his new trousers and his best shirt. But when Bella came, she told him she was going out with Kevin Clarke.

'But you promised –'

'I never promised, I just said I might,' she told him. 'Ask me again some time.'

So he asked her the next day, and the next day and the next, and every time she said, 'I dunno. I might. Ask me again.'

The last time she said this, he turned away without a word, and went to look out of the window, ignoring her. She didn't like that.

'What are you looking at?' she asked, coming to stand beside him.

'Nothing in particular.'

'Yes, you are. You're looking at Meg Hunter. Here she comes, late as usual. Doesn't she look stupid when she runs? Look at that smudge on her face! She can't have washed at all this morning.'

Edward knew how Meg got smudges on her face. Sometimes, when he was late, he saw her going along the road in front of him, trailing her fingers over the ledges of the buildings, stroking the dusty plastic dog outside the pet shop, then pushing her unruly hair back from her face with sooty hands.

'It's only dust,' he said.

'And what on earth does she think she's wearing? That cardigan's hideous! And it's coming unravelled at the sleeve. Why doesn't she make her stepmother buy her some decent clothes?'

'What she needs is a fairy godmother, a pumpkin and a prince,' Edward said.

'What she needs is a hot bath and a haircut,' Bella retorted, wrinkling her pretty little nose. 'Don't tell me you fancy her, Edward?'

Before he could answer, Mr Dunlock, their teacher, came into the room and ordered them to their places. Edward saw Meg, trying to slip unnoticed into the room, trip over someone's leg – whose? was it Bella's? – and stumble heavily against one of the tables.

'Late again, Meg?' Mr Dunlock said. He peered at her through his spectacles. 'What's that on your face? It looks like soot. Go and wash it off, there's a good girl.'

As Meg left the room, some of the girls giggled and whispered. Edward was too far away to see who they were. He wondered if Bella was one of them. She could be spiteful, he'd already found that out, but he didn't want to have to start again with another girl. He was used to being in love with her, used to asking her out, even used to being refused.

There was something to be said for unrequited love. It was safer. Often, in his sleep, when he tried to kiss Bella, he tripped over his own feet and missed her altogether. Once he dreamed he was sitting next to her in the dark cinema, holding her hand. But when he leaned over to kiss her, she suddenly turned into Mrs Trenter, their head teacher, who shouted angrily, 'Edward Walden, you've failed your tests! What will your mother say?'

Nevertheless it hurt his pride that Bella should keep on refusing him when she went out with several other boys who were not, he considered, better looking or more amusing or in any way nicer than he was.

'I don't mean to be conceited, but honestly!' he said to his friend Michael. 'She's been out with Kevin a lot, and he's the dregs. Why do you think it is?'

'The girl's daft,' Michael said kindly. 'She's got bad taste.'

The next Sunday, Edward walked moodily in the park, looking for Meg. He found her sitting in her favourite tree and climbed up beside her.

'Do you think there's something wrong with me?' he asked.

'In what way? Have you got a pain or spots or something?'

'No. I meant . . . Am I off-putting in any way? Have I got halitosis or do my feet stink?'

'No,' she said.

'If you were Bella, would you rather go out with me or Kevin Clarke?'

Meg laughed. 'Kevin Clarke writes her poems,' she said.

'Poems?' Edward repeated in astonishment. 'Whatever for?'

'She likes them. She sticks them in an album opposite photographs of herself, and shows them to us.'

'Good grief,' Edward said, appalled by this new slant on his beloved. 'What are they about?'

'They're all about her, of course,' Meg told him. 'You know the sort of thing:

> *'Oh, Bella's hair is brighter than the sun,*
> *And Bella's eyes are bluer than the sky –'*

'What rot!' Edward said in disgust. 'It's not even true. Bella's hair is pretty enough, but I bet it's never ripened any tomatoes. I wonder she can stomach such tripe. She must be terribly vain.'

Meg didn't say anything.

'*You* wouldn't want anyone to write poems to you, would you, Meg?' he asked.

'I don't know. Just once, perhaps. But nobody ever will,' she said. He thought she sounded a bit wistful.

'I'll write you a poem, if you like,' he offered. 'Not that I'm any good at it, but I bet I can do as well as Kevin. Shall I?'

'Don't say that my hair will ripen tomatoes because it won't,' she said, pushing it back from her face and leaving a smudge on her nose. 'It might do to plant mustard and cress in. Mum's always trying to persuade me to have it cut.'

'I shall be strictly truthful,' he promised.

'Oh dear.'

After a moment, he began:

> *'Your hair is rough and long and needs a cut,*
> *Your eyes are . . .'*

'What colour are your eyes, Meg? I can't remember. Look at me, please.'

She turned her head. Her eyes were a greenish hazel and very bright. They reminded him of the sea at Cosheston, sparkling over the pebbles in the sunlight . . .

> *'Your mermaid eyes are flecked with gold and green.*
> *Your nose is smudged, your sleeve unravelled but*
> *Of all the girls at school you are my queen.'*

He shouldn't have said that last line. It wasn't true, was it? What about Bella? Besides, he couldn't date Meg. His mother would have a fit and everybody at school would tease him. He looked at her anxiously, hoping she wouldn't take it seriously, but she only laughed and told him it was a splendid poem, far better than any of Kevin's.

'Don't worry,' she said. 'I won't tell Bella.'

At the end of term, their school had a summer disco in the assembly hall. Edward didn't think he'd go. He had given up asking Bella to come out with him, and no longer dreamed of her at night. So he was surprised when she came up to him and said, 'Aren't you going to ask if you can take me to the summer disco, Edward?'

'You don't need anyone to go with. You can just go,' he told her.

'I know that,' she said. 'I just thought you might want to call for me so we could go together.'

He looked at her suspiciously. 'Would you come with me if I asked you?'

'I dunno. I might,' she said and ran off, giggling.

'And I might ask some other girl,' he said, and walked off. He knew whom he was going to ask. It was only when he found Meg in the library that it occurred to him that she might refuse.

'Please,' he asked, as she hesitated.

'I thought you'd ask Bella Jones,' she said.

'No, I'm asking you.'

'I can't dance,' she said. 'I've never been to a disco.'

'Nor have I,' he told her and they smiled at one another.

He was nervous, standing outside the school on the Saturday of the party. Sometimes he was afraid Meg would not come after all, and Bella would laugh. Sometimes he was afraid Meg would come in her old green trousers, still done up with a safety pin, with her hair unbrushed and her face smudged, and Bella would laugh even louder. Bella had arrived with Kevin Clarke, and they were waiting in the entrance, looking at him and sniggering; Bella with her yellow hair frizzed out and her claws sharpened.

'Who are you waiting for, Edward?' she called out, but just then a big silver car drew up outside the school gates, and a girl in a sea-green dress got out. Her long brown hair was sleek and shining, earrings sparkled in her ears and there were silver buckles on her shoes. As she walked towards them, the thin material of her dress swirled out like the waves of the sea.

Everyone stared.

'Meg,' Edward said, coming forward. 'Meg, you look fabulous.'

'Don't I look posh? I hardly know myself,' she told him, laughing. 'Mum and my sisters took me in hand. They've been longing to do it for ages, but I wouldn't let them. Mum's bought me a whole lot of new clothes. Josie gave me these earrings and Netta these bracelets.'

She was no Cinderella, after all. She was Meg, whose family loved her, enough to let her play football in the park and climb trees when she wanted to, and to do her proud when the time came. She's beautiful, he thought, and felt for a moment an odd pang of loss. Had she gone for good, the laughing, untidy, romping girl who'd not wanted to grow up?

'Don't change too much,' he said. Then, as she looked up at him, he noticed a small smudge of eyeblack on her left cheek. Without thinking, he bent down and kissed her, forgetting that Bella and her friends were watching until he heard the catcalls. He didn't care what they thought, not now. It was as if the kiss had broken a spell and set him free. Nobody was going to tell him what to think any longer, nor choose his friends for him. This was the girl he had always liked. The others could suit themselves.

Gift
Susan Gates

I'm standing at the turn-off with Gift Mlungu. We're waiting for the bus to his village. It's a long way away, up country.

Gift is our school's champion sprinter. When he runs in his shorts and PE vest, it makes me trembly inside. He's got speed like a leopard, grace like a gazelle.

My friend Gracie Kainja said, 'Eeeee, he is one sweet guy!'

His nickname is *gudji-gudji* – after a spider that runs like lightning. It's got a body flat as a penny and long racehorse legs. But I don't call him *gudji-gudji*. I call him Gift.

He's tall and slender and proud – like a Zulu even though that's not his tribe. He's seventeen, two years older than me. And I didn't think he even noticed me.

Until two weeks ago, that is, when he said, 'How about spending some days at my house, in the holidays?'

I couldn't believe it! 'Are you sure?' I asked him. 'You want *me* to come to *your* house?'

'I have just said so,' he told me.

So I asked Mum and she said yes.

So here we are, Gift and me, waiting for the bus. There are children watching us from the doorways of huts, from under the mango trees. Some are peeping at us between high elephant grass.

I'm an *azungu* – a white person. I'm the only white pupil at St Martin's school. My mum and dad are teachers here, in Africa. So I go to St Martin's, where they teach. It's a boarding school because most kids come from faraway villages. Too far to go home, except in the holidays. And I don't sleep in Mum and Dad's house. I sleep in the school dormitory with all my friends.

Most times I forget I'm white. When I comb my hair in the dormitory mirror, I think, 'Hey, how did that *azungu* get in here?'

As we wait at the bus stop, I ask Gift, 'Are those children staring at me because I'm an *azungu* ?'

Gift laughs. 'No, they are staring at me, because I am so beautiful, in my best clothes!'

Gift's not in school uniform today. He's got a blue denim shirt on and brilliant white jeans. I'm in love. Gracie, my friend, once said to me, 'I tell you, girl, I have got the hots for that guy! He is the handsomest guy in this school!'

She's right. I've got the hots for him too. I'm standing beside him with a great big grin on my face. That's because it's only just hit me. Gift picked me. Me! Over all the beautiful girls in our school. Take Gracie for instance; she looks fantastic dressed up in her red and blue *zambia* with beads plaited into her hair. She looks so tall and elegant.

But he didn't choose Gracie. He chose me. Every time I think about that I think, Wow! And it feels like meltdown inside my heart.

There's an orange dust cloud creeping towards us up the road. 'Here's the bus!' I tell Gift. I'm really excited.

There are loads of bicycles strapped on the roof. It's going to be crowded! Inside I have to fight my way through baskets of dried fish and green bananas and squawking chickens to find a seat. It's so crowded I can't sit with Gift. I'm next to an old mama, eating sugar cane. She breaks off a piece for me.

'Try! Try!' she says to me, in English.

So I say, in her language, '*Moni, Mama, muli bwanji* !' Which means, How are you?

'*Eeeee!* ' she shrieks in surprise. 'You are white, but you speak like an African.'

I really like it when she says that.

Most of the time I look out at the tea fields. But I keep taking sneaky glances at Gift. I can see him laughing with people at the front of the bus. He's so good-looking, I'm so proud to be with him. I wish he'd glance at me just once. I keep saying inside my head, Look at me Gift, just look at me, as if my mind can speak to his mind. When he looks I'm going to give him my best smile. But he doesn't look – it doesn't matter. He's invited me to his house, to meet his parents. That means I'm his special girl.

While we were waiting at the bus stop I said to Gift, 'Do you have many brothers and sisters?'

It's funny, I don't know much about him, even though I'm his special girl.

'Oh, many!' laughed Gift. 'Many little sisters and brothers! I cannot count them! You will trip over them. They will drive you crazy!'

Gift's mother is waiting for us when we get off the bus. She's shy and doesn't speak English. She has a baby boy on her back.

'*Muli bwanje?*' I ask her. I give her my best smile. I smile and smile until my jaw aches. I want to make a good impression. I really want Gift's family to like me.

The baby has a string of blue glass beads round his neck. He's eating a passion fruit. The pink juice is dribbling down his chin. I grin at the baby.

'Is this your brother?' I ask Gift.

'Ya, this one's name is Bernard,' says Gift.

The baby peeps over his mother's shoulder. He notices me for the first time. I flash him an extra big smile. He screams! He screams blue murder, as if I'm a monster or something. He buries his face in his mother's dress.

I'm really, really upset. 'Gift, what's wrong with him?'

Gift laughs, 'Oh, don't worry. He has never seen an *azungu*. Not many *azungus* come this far north. He is frightened of you, that's all.'

But I'm still upset. I feel like running away and hiding. I don't like scaring babies. And I don't like being singled out as an *azungu*. Like I said before, until I look in the dormitory mirror, I forget that I'm different.

But Gift just shrugs and laughs. And when he laughs everything is wonderful. His face is like sunshine. And I think, It will be OK. The baby will get used to me.

I'm longing to be on my own with Gift. I'm really impatient, I can't wait. I mean, that's what he brought me here for, isn't it? So we can be alone together? But his family are always around. His little sisters are always in the way. I'm sharing a bedroom with three of them.

When it's bedtime, they don't go to sleep. They sit in a row on their iron cot, just staring at me with big round eyes.

'Where's Gift?' I ask them. 'I want to see Gift.' I haven't seen him since teatime. But they just giggle.

I've got my own bed. But it's embarrassing getting undressed. They stare and stare, like I'm a freak show or something. I try to get undressed under my nightshirt. I pull off my white pants.

'*Aiee*!' cries the littlest one and runs out the door. She's screaming something in her own language but I don't know it well enough to understand what she's saying.

The two other sisters go crazy. They fall about on the bed. They shake with laughter.

'What's wrong with her?' I ask them.

'*Cha*, she is so stupid,' says the biggest one. 'She does not understand. She thinks you are taking off your white skin, like a snake! She thinks you are taking off your white skin and you will just be a skeleton underneath!'

And they both laugh themselves silly.

But I'm not laughing. I'm angry and upset. I don't understand. I don't want to scare anyone. I just want to belong. I wish Gift was here. I feel lonely, even a bit weepy. And I'm thinking, I shouldn't have come here. It was a big mistake.

I can't sleep. The little sisters are asleep, all in a heap like a nest of puppies. But I'm awake, staring at the ceiling, thinking about Gift. There are two geckos running round up there – girlfriend and boyfriend. They're batting their eyelids at each other. They're transparent and inside their bodies, you can see their little beating hearts.

In the morning, things look a lot better. I tell myself, You were tired last night. From that long, hot bus trip.

The baby doesn't howl when he sees me. The littlest sister doesn't run away. We have maize porridge for breakfast. Gift's mother is really nice. And Gift is smiling that drop-dead gorgeous smile that makes me weak at the knees. I'm really glad I came.

'I will show you my village,' says Gift.

Great! *At last* I'm spending some time with him. On my own. We were never alone at school. Not once. There were always other kids around. And anyway, I only saw him during the day. At night boys can't visit the girls' dormitories. That's a very strict rule at St Martin's.

Gift's village is just the same as lots of other villages. There's nothing much to see. Just one street with some Indian shops.

But I don't care. Because I'm walking with Gift. Me and him together. I'm so in love I'm dizzy. It's like I'm floating – like walking on bubbles, not on the hard, dusty ground.

Gift shows me a field with yellow dried-up grass. 'That is our football field,' he says.

We buy a can of Fanta and share it. The Fanta's sickly and warm but I don't care.

He shows me a white hut with a tin roof. 'That is where I went to primary school. Mr Austin Jawali was our teacher.'

And I'm thinking, When is he going to kiss me? If he doesn't do it soon, I'll have to kiss him first.

And I'm just daring myself to do it when Gift says, 'I want to introduce you to someone.'

He goes into an Indian shop. I follow him inside. When my eyes get used to the dark, I see that the shop sells saris. There's lots of cloth on the shelves. Some of it is gold and silver, for wedding saris.

Gift says to someone. 'Here is our English guest from St Martin's. Her mother and father are teachers there.'

I wonder why he says 'our English guest' instead of 'my girlfriend'. But I'm too busy looking for who he's talking to. Then I see her – the Indian lady behind the counter. She's eating slices of fried cassava, dipping them in salt. She smiles at me. Beside her is a girl in a blue sari. She's about my age. She's got big gentle eyes, like a deer. She's got gold bangles all the way up her arms. And she's very, very beautiful.

Gift turns to me. 'This is Sunni,' he says. 'My future bride. And this is her mother.'

I forget to be polite. I can't say a thing. Words would choke me.

My brain's racing fast as a *gudji-gudji*. I don't understand. I *won't* understand!

'Go, go,' says Sunni's mother, shooing us into the back room like chickens. 'Go, Sunni. You may help Gift entertain his English guest. Give her tea. After all, it is quite proper. You will not be alone together. The English guest will be your chaperone.'

And now it's like I'm in a trance. It's dark in the back room. Sunni and Gift sit me down on this pink plastic settee. There's a fan going round, *clunk, clunk, clunk* in the ceiling.

Gift says, 'We will not be long.'

And he and Sunni disappear into another room.

Even then I'm trying to deny it.

But there's an oil lamp alight in the other room. And for a minute I see them, like big shadow puppets on the wall. I see her lifting her shadow face up to him. I see the two shadows kiss, so gently and tenderly.

And I can't deny it any more.

I sit waiting and waiting. It's hot. My dress is sticking to the plastic settee. But I'm frozen inside with misery. And all the time, over my head, the fan is going *clunk, clunk, clunk*, in the ceiling . . .

So that's it then. I finally understand. For the rest of my stay at Gift's we all go out together, Sunni and Gift and me, every day, in a threesome. Everyone is very nice. But Sunni and Gift share a can of Fanta. They whisper together. They giggle. They snatch kisses. They're desperate to be alone. So I walk a long way behind them. The English guest – a perfect chaperone.

They're in love. They're crazy about each other. Anyone can see that. I don't blame Gift. I was a fool, I didn't understand. Didn't want to understand. But that doesn't stop my heart from breaking. He was one sweet guy.

Thank God I didn't kiss him. I would have felt an even bigger fool. But I didn't. And, of course, I'll never do it now.

When I get back to St Martin's I say to Gracie, 'I didn't know Gift was going to be married.'

'Oh yes,' said Gracie. 'When he is eighteen. Did you meet her? She is Muslim, like Gift. They have been promised to each other for a long, long time. Ever since they were children. It is a family arrangement. Did you not know? Your mother knows. Everybody knows.'

So why did nobody tell *me*?

But it's my own fault. I didn't understand. I thought I understood Africa. But I've got such a lot to learn.

I still wonder why Gift asked me to his village. Was it just to be a chaperone? So Sunni and he could spend time together without her mother kicking up a fuss? Or did he like me, just a bit? Still, it doesn't matter now. He loves Sunni, and not me and I mustn't dream about him any more.

I'll get over Gift. Course I will. There are other boys I like. One asked me to dance at the school dance last Saturday.

But you ought to see him running. When he comes powering home, burning up the track, my heart still goes, *ping!* I can't help it.

And now and again, I feel a bit weepy. Especially when I see two geckos on the dormitory wall, girlfriend and boyfriend, with their little hearts beating like mad.

Science fiction

Science fiction can stretch the imagination further than you might have thought possible, as the two stories in this section show. More than 100 years ago, authors were writing about time travel, space travel and meetings with aliens, and these themes are still present in this genre today.

A Sound of Thunder – Ray Bradbury
Ray Bradbury is one of the most important writers of science fiction and fantasy in the twentieth century. He was born in America in 1920 and started writing short stories when he was just a child. This story is set in the future. It demonstrates some of the common features of the science fiction genre, particularly in the setting and its use of technical language. See if you can pinpoint these as you read through the story.

Mind Bend – Martin Martinsen
As is typical of science fiction this story is set on another planet in the future. As you read the story consider how the technical language and futuristic setting help you to believe in this other-worldly place.

A Sound of Thunder
Ray Bradbury

The sign on the wall seemed to quaver under a film of sliding warm water. Eckels felt his eyelids blink over his stare, and the sign burned in this momentary darkness:

TIME SAFARI, INC.
SAFARIS TO ANY YEAR IN THE PAST.
YOU NAME THE ANIMAL.
WE TAKE YOU THERE.
YOU SHOOT IT.

A warm phlegm gathered in Eckels' throat; he swallowed and pushed it down. The muscles around his mouth formed a smile as he put his hand slowly out upon the air, and in that hand waved a check for ten thousand dollars to the man behind the desk.

'Does this safari guarantee I come back alive?'

'We guarantee nothing,' said the official, 'except the dinosaurs.' He turned. 'This is Mr Travis, your Safari Guide in the Past. He'll tell you what and where to shoot. If he says no shooting, no shooting. If you disobey instructions, there's a stiff penalty of another ten thousand dollars, plus possible government action, on your return.'

Eckels glanced across the vast office at a mass and tangle, a snaking and humming of wires and steel boxes, at an aurora that flickered now orange, now silver, now blue. There was a sound like a gigantic bonfire burning all of Time, all the years and all the parchment calendars, all the hours piled high and set aflame.

A touch of the hand and this burning would, on the instant, beautifully reverse itself. Eckels remembered the wording in the advertisements to the letter. Out of chars and ashes, out of dust and coals, like golden salamanders, the old years, the green years, might leap; roses sweeten the air, white hair turn Irish-black, wrinkles vanish; all, everything fly back to seed, flee death, rush down to their beginnings, suns rise in western skies and set in glorious easts, moons eat themselves opposite to the custom, all and everything cupping one in another like Chinese boxes, rabbits in hats, all and everything returning to the fresh death, the seed death, the green death, to the time before the beginning. A touch of a hand might do it, the merest touch of a hand.

'Hell and damn,' Eckels breathed, the light of the Machine on his thin face. 'A real Time Machine.' He shook his head. 'Makes you think. If the election had gone badly yesterday, I might be here now running away from the results. Thank God Keith won. He'll make a fine President of the United States.'

'Yes,' said the man behind the desk. 'We're lucky. If Deutscher had gotten in, we'd have the worst kind of dictatorship. There's an anti-everything man for you, a militarist, anti-Christ, anti-human, anti-intellectual. People called us up, you know, joking but not joking. Said if Deutscher became President they wanted to go live in 1492. Of course it's not our business to conduct Escapes, but to form Safaris. Anyway, Keith's President now. All you got to worry about is –'

'Shooting my dinosaur,' Eckels finished it for him.

'A *Tyrannosaurus rex*. The Thunder Lizard, the damnedest monster in history. Sign this release. Anything happens to you, we're not responsible. Those dinosaurs are hungry.'

Eckels flushed angrily. 'Trying to scare me!'

'Frankly, yes. We don't want anyone going who'll panic at the first shot. Six Safari leaders were killed last year, and a dozen hunters. We're here to give you the damnedest thrill a *real* hunter ever asked for. Travelling you back sixty million years to bag the biggest damned game in all Time. Your personal check's still there. Tear it up.'

Mr Eckels looked at the check for a long time. His fingers twitched.

'Good luck,' said the man behind the desk. 'Mr Travis, he's all yours.'

They moved silently across the room, taking their guns with them, toward the Machine, toward the silver metal and the roaring light.

First a day and then a night and then a day and then a night, then it was day-night-day-night-day. A week, a month, a year, a decade! AD 2055. AD 2019. 1999! 1957! Gone! The Machine roared.

They put on their oxygen helmets and tested the intercoms.

Eckels swayed on the padded seat, his face pale, his jaw stiff. He felt the trembling in his arms and he looked down and found his hands tight on the new rifle. There were four other men in the Machine. Travis, the Safari Leader, his assistant, Lesperance, and two other hunters, Billings and Kramer. They sat looking at each other, and the years blazed around them.

'Can these guns get a dinosaur cold?' Eckels felt his mouth saying.

'If you hit them right,' said Travis on the helmet radio. 'Some dinosaurs have two brains, one in the head, another far down the spinal column. We stay away from those. That's stretching luck. Put your first two shots into the eyes, if you can, blind them, and go back into the brain.'

The Machine howled. Time was a film run backward. Suns fled and ten million moons fled after them. 'Good God,' said Eckels. 'Every hunter that ever lived would envy us today. This makes Africa seem like Illinois.'

The Machine slowed; its scream fell to a murmur. The Machine stopped.

The sun stopped in the sky.

The fog that had enveloped the Machine blew away and they were in an old time, a very old time indeed, three hunters and two Safari Heads with their blue metal guns across their knees.

'Christ isn't born yet,' said Travis. 'Moses has not gone to the mountain to talk with God. The Pyramids are still in the earth, waiting to be cut out and put up. *Remember* that, Alexander, Caesar, Napoleon, Hitler – none of them exists.'

The men nodded.

'That' – Mr Travis pointed – 'is the jungle of sixty million two thousand and fifty-five years before President Keith.'

He indicated a metal path that struck off into green wilderness, over steaming swamp, among giant ferns and palms.

'And that,' he said, 'is the Path, laid by Time Safari for your use. It floats six inches above the earth. Doesn't touch so much as one grass blade, flower, or tree. It's an antigravity metal. Its purpose is to keep you from touching this world of the past in any way. Stay on the Path. Don't go off it. I repeat. *Don't go off.* For *any* reason! If you fall off, there's a penalty. And don't shoot any animal we don't okay.'

'Why?' asked Eckels.

They sat in the ancient wilderness. Far birds' cries blew on a wind, and the smell of tar and an old salt sea, moist grasses, and flowers the colour of blood.

'We don't want to change the Future. We don't belong here in the Past. The government doesn't *like* us here. We have to pay big graft to keep our franchise. A Time Machine is damn finicky business. Not knowing it, we might kill an important animal, a small bird, a roach, a flower even, thus destroying an important link in a growing species.'

'That's not clear,' said Eckels.

'All right,' Travis continued, 'say we accidentally kill one mouse here. That means all the future families of this one particular mouse are destroyed, right?'

'Right.'

'And all the families of the families of that one mouse! With a stamp of your foot, you annihilate first one, then a dozen, then a thousand, a million, a *billion* possible mice!'

'So they're dead,' said Eckels. 'So what?'

'So what?' Travis snorted quietly. 'Well, what about the foxes that'll need those mice to survive? For want of ten mice, a fox dies. For want of ten foxes, a lion starves. For want of a lion, all manner of insects, vultures, infinite billions of life forms are thrown into chaos and destruction. Eventually it all boils down to this: fifty-nine million years later, a cave man, one of a dozen on the *entire* world, goes hunting wild boar or sabre-tooth tiger for food. But you, friend, have *stepped* on all the tigers in that region. By stepping on *one* single mouse. So the cave man starves. And the cave man, please note, is not just *any* expendable man, no! He is an *entire future nation*. From his loins would have sprung ten sons. From *their* loins one hundred sons, and thus onward to a civilisation. Destroy this one man, and you destroy a race, a people, an entire history of life. It is comparable to slaying some of Adam's grandchildren. The stomp of your foot, on one mouse, could start an earthquake, the effects of which could shake our earth and destinies down through Time, to their very foundations. With the death of that one cave man, a billion others yet unborn are throttled in the womb. Perhaps Rome never rises on its seven hills. Perhaps Europe is forever a dark forest, and only Asia waxes healthy and teeming. Step on a mouse and you crush the Pyramids. Step on a mouse and you leave your print, like a Grand Canyon, across Eternity. Queen Elizabeth might never be born, Washington might not cross the Delaware, there might never be a United States at all. So be careful. Stay on the Path. *Never* step off!'

'I see,' said Eckels. 'Then it wouldn't pay for us even to touch the *grass*?'

'Correct. Crushing certain plants could add up infinitesimally. A little error here would multiply in sixty million years, all out of proportion. Of course maybe our theory is wrong. Maybe Time *can't* be changed by us. Or maybe it can be changed only in little subtle ways. A dead mouse here makes an insect imbalance there, a population disproportion later, a bad harvest further on, a depression, mass starvation, and, finally, a change in *social* temperament in far-flung countries. Something much more subtle, like that. Perhaps only a soft breath, a whisper, a hair, pollen on the air, such a slight, slight change that unless you looked close you wouldn't see it. Who knows? Who really can say he knows? We don't know. We're guessing. But until we do know for certain whether our messing around in Time *can* make a big roar or a little rustle in history, we're being damned careful. This Machine, this Path, your clothing and bodies, were sterilised, as you know, before the journey. We wear these oxygen helmets so we can't introduce our bacteria into an ancient atmosphere.'

'How do we know which animals to shoot?'

'They're marked with red paint,' said Travis. 'Today, before our journey, we sent Lesperance here back with the Machine. He came to this particular era and followed certain animals.'

'Studying them?'

'Right,' said Lesperance. 'I track them through their entire existence, noting which of them lives longest. Very few. How many times they mate. Not often. Life's short. When I find one that's going to die when a tree falls on him, or one that drowns in a tar pit, I note the exact hour, minute, and second. I shoot a paint bomb. It leaves a red patch on his hide. We can't miss it. Then I correlate our arrival in the Past so that we meet the Monster not more than two minutes before he would have died anyway. This way, we kill only animals with no future, that are never going to mate again. You see how *careful* we are?'

'But if you came back this morning in Time,' said Eckels eagerly, 'you must've bumped into *us*, our Safari! How did it turn out? Was it successful? Did all of us get through – alive?'

Travis and Lesperance gave each other a look.

'That'd be a paradox,' said the latter. 'Time doesn't permit that sort of mess – a man meeting himself. When such occasions threaten, Time steps aside. Like an airplane hitting an air pocket. You felt the Machine jump just before we stopped? That was us passing ourselves on the way back to the Future. We saw nothing. There's no way of telling *if* this expedition was a success, *if* we got our monster, or whether all of – meaning *you*, Mr Eckels – got out alive.'

Eckels smiled palely.

'Cut that,' said Travis sharply. 'Everyone on his feet!'

They were ready to leave the Machine.

The jungle was high and the jungle was broad and the jungle was the entire world forever and forever. Sounds like music and sounds like flying tents filled the sky, and those were pterodactyls soaring with cavernous gray wings, gigantic bats out of a delirium and a night fever. Eckels, balanced on the narrow Path, aimed his rifle playfully.

'Stop that!' said Travis. 'Don't even aim for fun, damn it! If your gun should go off –'

Eckels flushed. 'Where's our *Tyrannosaurus*?'

Lesperance checked his wrist watch. 'Up ahead. We'll bisect his trail in sixty seconds. Look for the red paint, for Christ's sake. Don't shoot till we give the word. Stay on the Path. *Stay on the Path!*'

They moved forward in the wind of morning.

'Strange,' murmured Eckels. 'Up ahead, sixty million years, Election Day over. Keith made President. Everyone celebrating. And here we are, a million years lost, and they don't exist. The things we worried about for months, a lifetime, not even born or thought about yet.'

'Safety catches off, everyone!' ordered Travis. 'You, first shot, Eckels. Second, Billings. Third, Kramer.'

'I've hunted tiger, wild boar, buffalo, elephant, but Jesus, this is *it*,' said Eckels. 'I'm shaking like a kid.'

'Ah,' said Travis.

Everyone stopped.

Travis raised his hand. 'Ahead,' he whispered. 'In the mist. There he is. There's His Royal Majesty now.'

The jungle was wide and full of twitterings, rustlings, murmurs, and sighs.

Suddenly it all ceased, as if someone had shut a door.

Silence.

A sound of thunder.

Out of the mist, one hundred yards away, came *Tyrannosaurus rex*.

'Jesus God,' whispered Eckels.

'Sh!'

It came on great oiled, resilient, striding legs. It towered thirty feet above half of the trees, a great evil god, folding its delicate watchmaker's claws close to its oily reptilian chest. Each lower leg was a piston, a thousand pounds of white bone, sunk in thick ropes of muscle, sheathed over in a gleam of pebbled skin like the mail of a terrible warrior. Each thigh was a ton of meat, ivory, and steel mesh. And from the great breathing cage of the upper body those two delicate arms dangled out front, arms with hands which might pick up and examine men like toys, while the snake neck coiled. And the head itself, a ton of sculptured stone, lifted easily upon the sky. Its mouth gaped, exposing a fence of teeth like daggers. Its eyes rolled, ostrich eggs, empty of all expression save hunger. It closed its mouth in a death grin. It ran, its pelvic bones crushing aside trees and bushes, its taloned feet clawing damp earth, leaving prints six inches deep wherever it settled its weight. It ran with a gliding ballet step, far too poised and balanced for its ten tons. It moved into a sunlit arena warily, its beautifully reptile hands feeling the air.

'My God!' Eckels twitched his mouth. 'It could reach up and grab the moon.'

'Sh!' Travis jerked angrily. 'He hasn't seen us yet.'

'It can't be killed.' Eckels pronounced this verdict quietly, as if there could be no argument. He had weighed the evidence and this was his considered opinion. The rifle in his hands seemed a cap gun. 'We were fools to come. This is impossible.'

'Shut up!' hissed Travis.

'Nightmare.'

'Turn around,' commanded Travis. 'Walk quietly to the Machine. We'll remit one-half your fee.'

'I didn't realize it would be this *big*,' said Eckels. 'I miscalculated, that's all. And now I want out.'

'It sees us!'

'There's the red paint on its chest!'

The Thunder Lizard raised itself. Its armoured flesh glittered like a thousand green coins. The coins, crusted with slime, steamed. In the slime, tiny insects wriggled, so that the entire body seemed to twitch and undulate, even while the monster itself did not move. It exhaled. The stink of raw flesh blew down the wilderness.

'Get me out of here,' said Eckels. 'It was never like this before. I was always sure I'd come through alive. I had good guides, good safaris, and safety. This time, I figured wrong. I've met my match and admit it. This is too much for me to get hold of.'

'Don't run,' said Lesperance. 'Turn around. Hide in the Machine.'

'Yes.' Eckels seemed to be numb. He looked at his feet as if trying to make them move. He gave a grunt of helplessness.

'Eckels!'

He took a few steps, blinking, shuffling.

'Not *that* way!'

The Monster, at the first motion, lunged forward with a terrible scream. It covered one hundred yards in four seconds. The rifles jerked up and blazed fire. A windstorm from the beast's mouth engulfed them in the stench of slime and old blood. The Monster roared, teeth glittering with sun.

Eckels, not looking back, walked blindly to the edge of the Path, his gun limp in his arms, stepped off the Path, and walked, not knowing it, in the jungle. His feet sank into green moss. His legs moved him, and he felt alone and remote from the events behind.

The rifles cracked again. Their sound was lost in shriek and lizard thunder. The great lever of the reptile's tail swung up, lashed sideways. Trees exploded in clouds of leaf and branch. The Monster twitched its jeweller's hands down to fondle at the men, to twist them in half, to crush them like berries, to cram them into its teeth and its screaming throat. Its boulder-stone eyes levelled with the men. They saw themselves mirrored. They fired at the metallic eyelids and the blazing black iris.

Like a stone idol, like a mountain avalanche, *Tyrannosaurus* fell. Thundering, it clutched trees, pulled them with it. It wrenched and tore the metal Path. The men flung themselves back and away. The body hit, ten tons of cold flesh and stone. The guns fired. The Monster lashed its armoured tail, twitched its snake jaws, and lay still. A fount of blood spurted from its throat. Somewhere inside, a sac of fluids burst. Sickening gushes drenched the hunters. They stood, red and glistening.

The thunder faded.

The jungle was silent. After the avalanche, a green peace. After the nightmare, morning.

Billings and Kramer sat on the pathway and threw up. Travis and Lesperance stood with smoking rifles, cursing steadily.

In the Time Machine, on his face, Eckels lay shivering. He had found his way back to the Path, climbed into the Machine.

Travis came walking, glanced at Eckels, took cotton gauze from a metal box, and returned to the others, who were sitting on the Path.

'Clean up.'

They wiped the blood from their helmets. They began to curse too. The Monster lay, a hill of solid flesh. Within, you could hear the sighs and murmurs as the furthest chambers of it died, the organs malfunctioning, liquids running a final instant from pocket to sac to spleen, everything shutting off, closing up forever. It was like standing by a wrecked locomotive or a steam shovel at quitting time, all valves being released or levered tight. Bones cracked; the tonnage of its own flesh, off balance, dead weight, snapped the delicate forearms, caught underneath. The meat settled, quivering.

Another cracking sound. Overhead, a gigantic tree branch broke from its heavy mooring, fell. It crashed upon the dead beast with finality.

'There.' Lesperance checked his watch. 'Right on time. That's the giant tree that was scheduled to fall and kill this animal originally.' He glanced at the two hunters. 'You want the trophy picture?'

'What?'

'We can't take a trophy back to the Future. The body has to stay right here where it would have died originally, so the insects, birds, and bacteria can get at it, as they were intended to. Everything in balance. The body stays. But we *can* take a picture of you standing near it.'

The two men tried to think, but gave up, shaking their heads.

They let themselves be led along the metal Path. They sank wearily into the Machine cushions. They gazed back at the ruined Monster, the stagnating mound, where already strange reptilian birds and golden insects were busy at the steaming armour.

A sound on the floor of the Time Machine stiffened them. Eckels sat there, shivering.

'I'm sorry,' he said at last.

'Get up!' cried Travis.

Eckels got up.

'Go out on that Path alone,' said Travis. He had his rifle pointed. 'You're not coming back in the Machine. We're leaving you here!'

Lesperance seized Travis' arm. 'Wait –'

'Stay out of this!' Travis shook his hand away. 'This son of a bitch nearly killed us. But it isn't *that* so much. Hell, no. It's his *shoes*! Look at them! He ran off the Path. My God, that *ruins* us! Christ knows how much we'll forfeit. Tens of thousands of dollars of insurance! We guarantee no one leaves the Path. He left it. Oh, the damn fool! I'll have to report to the government. They might revoke our licence to travel. God knows *what* he's done to Time, to History!'

'Take it easy, all he did was kick up some dirt.'

'How do we *know*?' cried Travis. 'We don't know anything! It's all a damn mystery! Get out there, Eckels!'

Eckels fumbled his shirt. 'I'll pay anything. A hundred thousand dollars!'

Travis glared at Eckels' checkbook and spat. 'Go out there. The Monster's next to the Path. Stick your arms up to your elbows in his mouth. Then you can come back with us.'

'That's unreasonable!'

'The Monster's dead, you yellow bastard. The bullets! The bullets can't be left behind. They don't belong in the Past; they might change something. Here's my knife. Dig them out!'

The jungle was alive again, full of the old tremorings and bird cries. Eckels turned slowly to regard the primeval garbage dump, that hill of nightmares and terror. After a long time, like a sleepwalker, he shuffled out along the Path.

He returned, shuddering, five minutes later, his arms soaked and red to the elbows. He held out his hands. Each held a number of steel bullets. Then he fell. He lay where he fell, not moving.

'You didn't have to make him do that,' said Lesperance.

'Didn't I? It's too early to tell.' Travis nudged the still body. 'He'll live. Next time he won't go hunting game like this. Okay.' He jerked his thumb wearily at Lesperance. 'Switch on. Let's go home.'

1492.　　1776.　　1812.

They cleaned their hands and faces. They changed their caking shirts and pants. Eckels was up and around again, not speaking. Travis glared at him for a full ten minutes.

'Don't look at me,' cried Eckels. 'I haven't done anything.'

'Who can tell?'

'Just ran off the Path, that's all, a little mud on my shoes – what do you want me to do – get down and pray?'

'We might need it. I'm warning you, Eckels, I might kill you yet. I've got my gun ready.'

'I'm innocent. I've done nothing!'

1999.　　2000.　　2055.

The Machine stopped.

'Get out,' said Travis.

The room was there as they had left it. But not the same as they had left it. The same man sat behind the same desk. But the same man did not quite sit behind the same desk.

Travis looked around swiftly. 'Everything okay here?' he snapped.

'Fine. Welcome home!'

Travis did not relax. He seemed to be looking at the very atoms of the air itself, at the way the sun poured through the one high window.

'Okay, Eckels, get out. Don't ever come back.'

Eckels could not move.

'You heard me,' said Travis. 'What're you *staring* at?'

Eckels stood smelling of the air, and there was a thing to the air, a chemical taint so subtle, so slight, that only a faint cry of his subliminal senses warned him it was there. The colours, white, gray, blue, orange, in the wall, in the furniture, in the sky beyond the window, were . . . were . . . And there was a *feel*. His flesh twitched. His hands twitched. He stood drinking the oddness with the pores of his body. Somewhere, someone must have been screaming one of those whistles that only a dog can hear. His body screamed silence in return. Beyond this room, beyond this wall, beyond this man who was not quite the same man seated at this desk that was not quite the same desk . . . lay an entire world of streets and people. What sort of world it was now, there was no telling. He could feel them moving there, beyond the walls, almost, like so many chess pieces blown in a dry wind . . .

But the immediate thing was the sign painted on the office wall, the same sign he had read earlier today on first entering.

Somehow, the sign had changed:

TYME SEFARI INC.
SEFARIS TU ANY YEER EN THE PAST.

YU NAIM THE ANIMALL.
WEE TAEK YOU THAIR.
YOU SHOOT ITT.

Eckels felt himself fall into a chair. He fumbled crazily at the thick slime on his boots. He held up a clod of dirt, trembling. 'No, it *can't* be. Not a *little* thing like that. No!'

Embedded in the mud, glistening green and gold and black, was a butterfly, very beautiful, and very dead.

'Not a little thing like *that*! Not a butterfly!' cried Eckels.

It fell to the floor, an exquisite thing, a small thing that could upset balances and knock down a line of small dominoes and then big dominoes and then gigantic dominoes, all down the years across Time. Eckels' mind whirled. It *couldn't* change things. Killing one butterfly couldn't be *that* important! Could it?

His face was cold. His mouth trembled, asking: 'Who – who won the presidential election yesterday?'

The man behind the desk laughed. 'You joking? You know damn well. Deutscher, of course! Who else? Not that damn weakling Keith. We got an iron man now, a man with guts, by God!' The official stopped. 'What's wrong?'

Eckels moaned. He dropped to his knees. He scrabbled at the golden butterfly with shaking fingers. 'Can't we,' he pleaded to the world, to himself, to the officials, to the Machine, 'can't we take it *back*, can't we *make* it alive again? Can't we start over? Can't we –'

He did not move. Eyes shut, he waited, shivering. He heard Travis breathe loud in the room; he heard Travis shift his rifle, click the safety catch, and raise the weapon.

There was a sound of thunder.

Mind Bend
Martin Martinsen

When we heard there was a Mindbender on the planet, I was the only one who wasn't scared.

I wasn't being brave – just ignorant.

It was dad who told us. He came home late and sat down in the kitchen. I was watching the screen for an interview with the delegation from New Athens – I'll explain about that in a minute – and my sister was doing her homework. I asked dad what he'd been doing that day. I always ask him, because the answer is usually interesting – he's a lieutenant with the Spaceport Police. Cool as an ice asteroid, he said, 'I interviewed a Mindbender.' My sister screamed and mum dropped a plate.

I said, 'What's a Mindbender?'

I didn't get an answer for a while, what with mum going on about how we would all be murdered in our beds and Lu – that's my smart-alec sister – making remarks about kids who never pay attention in school, not to mention dad telling the cooker what he wanted for supper and the newsreader mumbling away on the screen.

When things quietened down dad said, 'They live on a group of planets in the Fishtail Cluster, and they practise an ancient art called hypnotism.'

Lu said, 'They just stare at you with their big beautiful eyes and they can make you do anything they want.' She enjoys being frightened. She's always reading stories about ugly monsters terrorising frail, pretty girls – despite the fact that she's almost as tall as dad and about as frail as the hull of a spaceliner.

I wasn't about to take her word for it, so I said, 'Is that true, dad?'

'It doesn't have to be their eyes,' he said. 'They can mesmerise you with a spinning coin, or a flashing light. But yes, once they've put you in a trance, they can make you do just about anything.'

'Can they make you forget you've been hypnotised?' I said.

'Oh, yes. In fact, they can plant in your mind a command to do something hours after you've come out of the trance. Months after, some of them.'

'Aha! So how do you know the Mindbender didn't hypnotise you?' I said triumphantly.

He gave me that sort of sad look that means I'm not being as clever as I ought. 'You can figure that out for yourself,' he said.

His supper popped out of the cooker on to the table, and he started to eat. Mum said, 'They shouldn't be allowed to wander around. They're dangerous.'

'They're not allowed to wander around,' Lu said. 'They're confined to their home planets, unless they have a special pass.'

'Did he have a pass, dad?'

Dad nodded.

Mum said, 'So he could be out there on the street right now?'

Dad swallowed. 'No. He's confined to the Spaceport Hotel until we've confirmed his documents. I sent an ethergram to the Fishtail Cluster today.'

I was still wondering how he managed to interview the Mindbender without risking getting hypnotised. 'I know!' I said. 'You took another detective with you to make sure the Mindbender behaved himself.'

'Wrong. How would he know he hadn't hypnotised both of us?'

'Shoot.'

Lu said, 'What does he look like, dad?'

'Ten feet tall, with green skin, a tail, and eyes on stalks.'

'Ugh!'

I knew he was kidding. 'You're kidding,' I said.

'Yes. Sorry, Lu. He looks just like you and me, except for his eyes, which are abnormally large and multi-coloured. So I'm told, anyway.'

I said, 'What do you mean, so you're told? You interviewed him, didn't you?'

'Keep thinking.'

'You interviewed him, but you didn't see him?'

'Right.'

'You phoned him, and left the vision off.'

'Right.'

I had it then. 'That's why he couldn't have hypnotised you – because you couldn't see him!'

'Well done,' he said. 'Now let's try you out on a general knowledge question. What do boys of your age have to do at this time of night?'

'I know,' I said disgustedly. 'Go to bed.'

'Full marks, and good night.'

Lu went, 'Heearg, heearg,' which is her way of laughing. Myself, I didn't see the joke.

Next day my teacher broke down and started talking gibberish, like, 'The square root of the galaxy is a metallic chloride.' The supervisor called in a teacher repairman, who looked at me suspiciously and said, 'Have you been asking silly questions?'

'No.'

'They do, you know,' the repairman said to the supervisor. 'They ask the teacher a riddle, like "What is zero divided by zero?", just so that the machine will break down and they can have a day off school.'

'I've never done anything like that,' I said indignantly. It's true – I haven't. I never thought of it. But it's not a bad idea. I must remember it.

He got out his screwdriver and took the screen off, and a few minutes later my teacher was scattered all over the classroom floor in pieces.

'Have you got some project work you can get on with?' the supervisor asked me.

I was ahead of her. 'I'm doing a politics project on the Galactic Emperor. Could I go to the Spaceport Hotel and interview the delegation from New Athens?'

'That's a good idea,' she said. 'You can go there directly on the hoverbus. Be sure to return by lunchtime.'

I picked up a handful of voice reels and went out, followed by envious glances from the rest of the class, still stuck in front of their screens.

The Spaceport Hotel is big. That's because the port is my planet's main industry. I'd better explain. This is the only planet of a lonely star roughly in the middle of a ring-shaped galaxy – which is why it's called Halfway. On the rim, every planet big enough to have a spaceline runs flights to and from Halfway; so you can get from anywhere to anywhere else if you go via Halfway. It's like an interstellar bus depot. (Of course, a wealthy planetary system – like, say, Marguerita – has spaceflights direct to many planets in its section of the rim. But nobody has flights to every planet – not even Imperium, which is the centre of the Galactic Federation.)

So, the Spaceport Hotel is big. It's full of beings from various parts of the galaxy waiting for connecting flights to other parts of the galaxy. Most of the aliens breathe oxygen and walk on two legs, like you and me; those who breathe steam or live in a bath of boiling oil have special rooms in the hotel basement, unofficially called the Zoo.

I went into the lobby, got the room number from the reception computer, and called the Athenians on the house phone.

A rather unattractive face, with a big nose and weathered skin, filled the screen and said, 'Yes?'

I'd been rehearsing a little speech. 'Good morning, my name is Dani Smiff and I'm doing a school project on the Galactic Emperor and I would like to talk to you if you could possibly spare me a few minutes, please?' I said it all in one breath.

The guy smiled, which improved his appearance, and said, 'I'll speak to you, on one condition.'

'What?'

'You promise to talk more slowly.'

'You got it.'

'Come on up.'

'That's me at the door now.'

There were three of them, actually – two men and a woman – and they were a little weird, but only a little. Their room (they all shared the one) was like a fridge: they had the heat switched off and the windows wide open. They wore loose, floor-length garments of a coarse material that looked suspiciously as though it was made of real animal hair. I kept my thermal coat on over my plastic jumpsuit.

They sat down to talk to me, and I realized right off that they came from a very poor planet. Diplomats almost always have lots of money to throw around, but these guys were sitting in their hotel room talking to me instead of enjoying the expensive amusements the port provides for visitors. Also, they obviously weren't accustomed to heated homes – hence the open windows.

I said, 'Is it okay if I record your voices?' I took a reel out of my pocket.

They were very interested in it. These reels are small, about the size of a coin. Most of the reel consists of the receiver/transmitter: the tape itself is simply a very long organic molecule. To start it, you just press its top with your finger. You use it once then throw it away – we use hundreds of them at school.

Anyway, it was another thing they didn't have on their planet, so I gave them one, and the younger man fooled around with it for a while. The elder man said to me, 'What can we tell you?'

I put a new reel on the table and said, 'In school we're taught that the emperor has no real power any more, and that the galaxy is ruled by the Council of Planets. If this is right, why are you travelling hundreds of light-years to present your petition to the emperor?' (I'd rehearsed that, too.)

It was the woman who answered. 'New Athens is a low-technology planet,' she said. 'We grow crops and raise livestock by old-fashioned methods: no weather control, no mutated seeds, no robot harvesters. You'd probably say we're poor, although we're rich in music, theatre and poetry. But one thing's for sure: without spaceflight and without weapons of mass destruction, we're vulnerable to invaders.'

'Anybody in particular?'

'Hondo,' said the younger man, and there was hatred in his voice. He lost interest in the reel, and dropped it into a drawer. 'A neighbouring planet,' he explained. 'They've colonised our moon and are looking greedily at our world.'

'Why don't you go to the Council of Planets?' I asked.

'The Council has no jurisdiction over worlds that don't have spaceflight,' said the elder man.

'So what can the emperor do?'

'There's a law, nine hundred years old, under which *anybody* in the galaxy can approach the emperor and ask for his help. You simply have to knock three times on the palace gate and say, "O Emperor of the Galaxy, I petition thee." Of course, the law isn't much use, because the people who need it – planets without spaceflight – have difficulty actually getting to the palace. But it was never repealed – just forgotten.

'Now, the emperor is still commander-in-chief of the Imperial Fleet. We will simply ask him to send the Fleet to our world to defend us.'

I asked the obvious question. 'You say the law isn't much use, because the people who need it can't get to the palace. How did you people manage it?'

The woman said quietly, 'It cost our planet three harvests.'

I couldn't think of anything to say after that. I mean, when people have spent the total produce of a whole planet three years running to make a trip, you don't ask them how they like Halfway. I was kind of awestruck. (I don't know what they lived on while they were saving – stores, I suppose, and fresh air.)

So I pocketed my reel, wished them luck, and left.

On the way out I met the Mindbender.

At first I didn't recognise him. He rode down in the lift with me, an ordinary humanoid wearing a pale green suit and a pair of darkened spectacles which hid his eyes. He got out in front of me and went to a drink dispenser in the lobby. Those machines are coin-operated. He took a handful of money from a pocket, and removed his glasses to find the right coins. That's when I saw his eyes.

They were incredible.

Spirals of colour radiated outwards from the small black pupils in the centre right to the edges – his eyes had no whites. Although he did not look at me, I could feel even indirectly the terrible desire to stare deeper into those whirlpools of colour. I tore my gaze away and hurried past him out to the hoverbus.

As a guest at the hotel, he had a perfectly good drink dispenser in his room, so he had no need to come down to the machine in the lobby. But that thought did not occur to me until later.

I was back in school for lunch. My teacher had been repaired, so I didn't play my recorded interview until later. When I got home, there was another reel waiting for me. It was the one I had given the Athenians. They had left it in their room when they departed, that afternoon, for Imperium. My name was on it, and the hotel manager likes to keep friendly with my father, so he had sent it around to our house by messenger.

At suppertime I made a bad mistake. I told dad I had seen the Mindbender. The mistake was to tell him while mum was in the room. She went bananas. I could have been killed, she said, and my school supervisor should be killed for letting me go, and by the time she began to run down dad was close to being killed for not getting as angry as mum about it.

'You're going to be locked in this house until that murdering creature has left the planet,' she finished up.

I appealed to dad.

'Fair enough,' he said. 'Dani stays in until the Mindbender has left.'

'Dad.'

'He left this afternoon,' dad said.

He likes playing tricks like that.

He explained, 'We sent him home, to the Fishtail Cluster. His documents were forged. He had a genuine pass to visit a planet in the Browning Loop; but instead of going straight home from there, he came to Halfway. The alterations he made to his pass looked pretty authentic, but when we checked with the Fishtail authorities they told us he had never been issued with the visas he showed us.' He paused, and frowned.

'Is that all?' I asked.

'I don't know,' he said. 'I'm surprised he got this far: the port police in the Browning Loop must be careless. But everybody knows we're very strict about documents here on Halfway. The Mindbender should have realised he'd never get away with it. So I wondered why he bothered to try.'

'Maybe he just wanted to see Planet Halfway,' I suggested.

'You're probably right.' When dad says that, it means I'm probably wrong. I felt like discussing the mysterious Mindbender some more, but I had homework to do. I went to my room and played the recording of my interview with the Athenians.

I noticed that the reel the hotel had returned to me had been used. Probably the younger Athenian had switched it on while fiddling with it, and left it on when he dropped it into the drawer.

Out of curiosity I played the tape. Although it was in the drawer, the reel had picked up the whole of my interview. I heard myself say good-bye and leave, then the woman said, 'Nice kid,' and one of the men said 'Yes.' Their phone buzzed, and the computer told them that their flight to Imperium would leave in three hours. For a while there were just footsteps and the sounds of people packing. The room door opened and shut a couple of times, meaning – I supposed – that two of them had gone out.

It occurred to me that I was eavesdropping, which is bad manners. I was about to switch the machine off and erase everything after the interview, when I heard a knock at the door of the hotel room. My finger hovered over the 'Stop' button. The door was opened, there was a grunt of surprise, and a voice said, 'Compliments of the management.' Someone entered the room. The strange voice said, 'Sleep.' I frowned: what was going on? Then the same voice said, 'Listen to me. You will kill the emperor when –'

And the reel ran out.

I stared at the machine. What did it mean? I played the last bit over again, trying to imagine it. There is one person left in the room. Someone knocks at the door, bringing some kind of gift from the hotel manager. The Athenian lets the stranger in. The stranger says 'Sleep', then tells the Athenian to kill the emperor . . .

I got an idea. I switched on my encyclopaedia and asked it where Planet Hondo was.

The encyclopaedia printed: PLANET HONDO. LARGEST PLANET IN THE BROWNING LOOP, IT ORBITS A G-TYPE STAR TO THE GALACTIC NORTH OF ARGEVIS ONE, ON –

I switched it off, found dad, and said, 'I think I know why the Mindbender came to Halfway.'

He sat and listened to the tape. When it finished he asked me to play it again. Then he said, 'What do *you* make of it?'

I took a deep breath. 'The Mindbender had a pass to a planet in the Browning Loop, you said. I think that planet was Hondo, the world that is about to invade New Athens. I think the Hondonians bribed the Mindbender to sabotage the Athenians' mission.'

'I think you're right. Go on.'

'The Mindbender came to Halfway. He knew he would meet the Athenians here, because everybody travels via Halfway. He knew you would check his documents and discover they were forged, but he didn't mind, so long as he had a little time here.

'While I was in the Spaceport Hotel, the Mindbender bought a tray of drinks in the lobby. He waited until one of the Athenians was alone, then went to their room with the drinks, pretending to be a live waiter – they're sure to have live waiters on a planet like Athens, it's a low-technology –'

'Yes, yes, I know.'

'Oh. Well, he got into the room and hypnotised one of the Athenians. When they reach Imperium, the hypnotised one will try to assassinate the emperor. People will think that was what they planned all the time, and instead of getting sympathy for their cause, they will turn the whole galaxy against them.'

Dad nodded. 'You've worked it out quite neatly,' he said. From him, that's high praise indeed. I couldn't help grinning with pleasure. Then he said, 'What do you think we should do?'

I liked the way he said 'we'. I thought for a minute. 'We have to find out *which* of the Athenians was hypnotised, and undo the conditioning.'

'How do we decide which one was hypnotised?'

I thought that was the easy part. 'Get the Mindbender back and make him tell us.'

'We can't get him back,' dad said. 'We've no proof he did anything more than forge documents.'

He was right.

He went on, 'Even if we get him back, there's no reason he should tell us anything; and if he told us something we wouldn't know whether it was true.'

I was stumped. 'What do *you* suggest?'

He frowned. 'We could get the delegation back.'

'No!' He looked at me, puzzled. I said, 'That would serve the Hondonians' purpose just as well. Besides, the Athenians' whole planet saved up for three years to pay for the trip.'

'Okay,' he said. 'We'll have to ask the Athenians a question. We'd better get going, so we can catch their ship before it goes into hyperspace.'

'What question?' I said. 'What question will we ask them?'

He grinned his most infuriating grin. 'See if you can work it out before we get there.'

Interstellar spaceliners go very fast, but they take a long time to build up speed. The ship the Athenians were on, the *Nova*, had left Halfway four hours ago, so it was still only a few million miles away. We got Space Traffic Control to beam a lasergram to the captain, saying: EMERGENCY EMERGENCY YOU HAVE ASSASSIN ON BOARD DECELERATE IMMEDIATELY AND PREPARE TO ADMIT PORT POLICE ACKNOWLEDGE ENDIT. We waited for the acknowledgement, then went out on to the blast pad.

We climbed aboard a high-speed police spaceyacht. We took with us Sergeant Hatcap, the best driver on the force, and my father's pal Lieutenant Bip, a sweaty, round-faced man who eats too much. Hatcap gave us a painful three gees to rip us away from Halfway's gravity, then we bulleted after the *Nova*.

It was my first time in deep space; previously I'd only been on the regular pleasure cruise around the moons. I can't tell you it was a big thrill: I felt groggy from the hard take-off and didn't get well until we locked trajectories with the *Nova*.

The big ship sprouted a tubular gangplank. It looked like one of those speeded-up films of a flower growing. We floated across under nil gravity, pulling ourselves by the grab handles along the walls of the tube. *Nova* had artificial gravity, and we sank to the floor gratefully.

Captain Gemman introduced himself and said, 'Now what's this all about?'

My father said, 'It concerns the three passengers from New Athens. If you would get them to meet us in the ship's library, I'll explain there.'

Captain Gemman shrugged. 'You're the boss. Give me five minutes.'

The library was a big circular room with racks of video reels on the walls and fifteen or twenty viewers placed in front of comfortable armchairs. There was also an antique book, made of paper, with the words printed on the paper in ink: it was in a glass case, and must have been a thousand years old.

Dad said, 'Have you figured out the question yet, Dani?'

'I think so,' I told him.

He grinned. 'You can ask it, then.'

The captain brought the Athenians in. They recognised me, and looked surprised and nervous. The captain spoke to my father. 'Lieutenant Smiff, I must ask you to do whatever you have to do as fast as possible – this delay is costing my company a small fortune.'

'Sure.' Dad told the story in a few sentences – he's good at summing things up. He finished, 'If you go on to Imperium in your present state, when you arrive you will be taken straight to a high-security hospital and kept there until the doctors have found out who has been hypnotised and then undone the conditioning. Mindbender conditioning is implanted so deep in the brain, and their understanding of hypnotism is so far in advance of anyone else's, that ordinary doctors could take goodness knows how long to sort it out.'

The elder Athenian held his head in his hands. 'Do we have an alternative?'

'Possibly. If we can find out here and now which of you is the assassin, then the other two will be able to see the emperor when you arrive.'

'How can we find out?' said the woman.

'I think there's a way,' dad said, and he looked at me.

I said, 'Which of you was left alone in the hotel room this afternoon?'

'I was,' said the woman. 'After you left, Dani, the other two went for a walk in the gardens. I must be the assassin.'

'That's it, then!' I said triumphantly.

'Just a minute,' said the younger man. 'When we came back from the gardens, she went to the shop in the lobby and he went out to check the baggage – so I was left alone, too.'

'So was I,' said the older Athenian. 'When we left, you two went ahead. I followed about fifteen minutes later.'

Dad sighed. 'So each of you was alone in the room at some time during the afternoon. We're back to square one.'

'There must be another way!' the younger man said.

Dad turned to Captain Gemman. 'Would you get the ship's doctor?'

The captain spoke into his pocket intercom. I wondered what my father was up to now. The doctor came immediately. She was a dark-skinned, stick-limbed woman from a low-gravity planet.

'Okay, lieutenant,' the captain said. 'Explain, please.'

'I have an idea,' dad said. 'It might not work, but it's worth a try. The problem is, what is the trigger? The Mindbender said, "You will kill the emperor *when* – ." When what? When you see him, perhaps. Or when he speaks, when you shake his hand, when he stands up, when he dismisses you . . . We just don't know. But if we can find that trigger, we can pull it and expose the assassin.'

'But we can't help you,' said the elder Athenian. 'The Mindbender must have hypnotised his victim to forget all about it until the crucial moment.'

'We've got to try and simulate that crucial moment,' dad said. 'This is my plan. We'll show you video reels of the emperor. The doctor here will give each of you an injection of psychobinol, a drug which will make you think the video pictures you see are real. If it works, one of you will try to kill the emperor on the screen, here in the library where you can do no harm. Are you willing?'

He looked at the three Athenians in turn, and each of them nodded.

While the doctor was giving them the drug, dad collected up all the weapons in sight: the cops' blasters, the sharp instruments from the doctor's case, a couple of heavy ornaments that were lying around, even Captain Gemman's ceremonial plasteel belt. He put them all in a pile outside the door.

The Athenians sat together in front of a large screen. The doctor looked at her watch and nodded. Dad plugged a reel into the machine, and we waited.

The reel was about tourist holidays on Planet Imperium. It started with a shot of the place from space, then zoomed in on the Imperial Palace. The camera moved slowly up the grand avenue and into the palace grounds. For the drugged Athenians, it must have been as if they were there.

We saw the marbled corridors of the ancient building, where each corner was the scene of some famous meeting, conspiracy, fight, or murder, and every wall was hung with priceless pictures and tapestries. Finally we got to the Old Palace, a single stone-walled room in the dead centre of the building. The heavy ornamental gate swung wide, and we saw the emperor.

The spaceship's library was very quiet. Dad was leaning forward in his chair, looking like a coiled spring. We all watched the Athenians.

Nothing happened.

The video showed the emperor greeting someone, talking, standing up, saying goodbye. It showed him signing papers, waving from windows, making speeches, inspecting his guard.

Nothing.

It showed him in close-up. He was younger than I expected, and had a perpetual wry smile, which seemed to say, 'This is all nonsense, but if they're prepared to pay me for doing it, why should I complain?' All his clothes were elaborate: multi-coloured things with ruffles and flares and slashes and all kinds of emblems.

The Athenians just sat still, gazing at the screen with the slightly dopey looks of drugged people.

The reel finished. Lieutenant Bip found a chocolate bar in his pocket and unwrapped it. Dad said, 'Obviously, it's not a visual thing, this trigger. But what else could it be? A smell, perhaps, or a touch, or something somebody says . . .'

Captain Gemman stood up. 'Lieutenant Smiff, it's our company's policy to co-operate with you people in every way possible; but we are now outside your jurisdiction, and I really cannot delay this spacecraft much longer. I think you're just going to have to take these Athenians back to Halfway.'

'Let me run the film once more,' dad said.

The captain sighed. 'Very well.'

Bip went to the video machine and restarted the reel. He said, 'If the Mindbender is clever – and he seems to be – he may have realised that the Athenians might watch a video reel like this before they got to Imperium. And it's possible that the reel might trigger the hypnosis even without the drug. So he would have been sensible enough to use a trigger which was unlikely to appear on film. In fact, the trigger should ideally be *something which can only happen when the Athenians meet the emperor*. A phrase, perhaps, like, "New Athens sends greetings to the Emperor of the Galaxy," or something.'

On the screen, the ceremonial gate of the Old Palace was opening. I remembered something. I said, 'When they reach this gate, they have to say: "O Emperor of the Galaxy, I petition thee." '

And that did it.

The younger Athenian man gave a blood-curdling scream and came up out of his seat in a blur. Hatcap and Bip went for blasters that weren't there. The Athenian's hand went inside his loose robe and came out holding a tiny narrow-beam laser. He took two steps toward the emperor's young face on the video screen. There was madness in his eyes as he thumbed the button. The laser hummed and glowed and spat a pencil beam of painfully bright light. It sliced across the video machine, cutting the emperor's image in half; then came back for another cut, and another, and another.

My father and Captain Gemman hit him at the same moment. The little laser flew upwards, cutting a streak across the ceiling before it faded off; and the Athenian went down under the combined weight of dad and the captain.

After a moment I came out from behind the chair.

'I had a feeling you might come up with the solution,' dad said to me. 'That's why I took you along.'

I glowed.

Now, in case nothing like this has ever happened to *you*, I have to tell you that it's bad for you. When an ordinary guy like you or me does something clever, he gets to thinking that maybe he's *not* so ordinary after all. But it doesn't last long, especially if you've got a father like mine.

We left the elder Athenian and the woman on the *Nova*, to continue their mission to Imperium. The younger man, who had been hypnotised, came back with us, and we checked him into the hospital to have his conditioning undone by Halfway's top neurosurgeon.

On the way home in a patrol car, dad said, 'So what are you going to tell everybody about what happened today?'

I looked at him. 'That I saved the emperor's life. I did, didn't I?'

He nodded. 'That's fine,' he said. It's one of his phrases that always means the opposite of what it says. I waited for the 'but'.

He said, 'But how will you explain why you were listening to a recording made secretly?'

'The reel I left in the Athenians' hotel room? But that was an accident.'

'Listening to it wasn't an accident,' he said. 'It was just bad manners.'

'I could say . . .' I didn't know what I could say.

'You could say you did wrong,' he told me.

So now you know. I did wrong.

They never let up, do they?

Horror stories

The final section of this collection of short stories gives two examples of the horror genre. As with many of the 'pairings' in this book, here we have a 'traditional' version of the theme, followed by a much more contemporary tale. You might like to note any differences or similarities as you read them.

The Tomb of Sarah – F G Loring

Ever since the famous nineteenth-century novel *Dracula* by Bram Stoker revived an old superstition about vampires, this theme has been a large part of the horror genre. It has its own traditions based on folk tales and legends of vampires from many cultures throughout the world. As you read this story see if you can notice many of the superstitions about vampires. You never know when your knowledge might come in useful!

Interview with the Vampire (extract) – Anne Rice

When the readers of the original vampire stories of the nineteenth and early twentieth century read about these superstitions they would have been very frightened by what they were told. In the twenty-first century we are perhaps more cynical about this kind of horror. Modern horror is often only loosely based on the more traditional religious ideas of the originals. Anne Rice's *Interview with the Vampire* gives a modern perspective on the vampire myth, and was made into a horror film in the modern setting of San Francisco. It starred Tom Cruise and Brad Pitt. As you read the story see if you are able to pinpoint the ways in which the vampire traditions have been modernised.

The Tomb of Sarah
F G Loring

Father was the head of a celebrated firm of church restorers and decorators about sixty years ago. He took a keen interest in his work, and made an especial study of any legends or family histories that came under his observation. He was necessarily very well read and thoroughly well posted in all questions of folk-lore and medieval legend. As he kept a careful record of every case he investigated the manuscripts he left at his death have a special interest. From amongst them I have selected the following, as being a particularly weird and extraordinary experience. In presenting it to the public I feel it is superfluous to apologise for its supernatural character.

SARAH 1630

FOR THE SAKE OF THE DEAD AND THE WELFARE OF THE LIVING, LET THIS SEPULCHRE REMAIN UNTOUCHED AND ITS OCCUPANT UNDISTURBED UNTIL THE COMING OF CHRIST IN THE NAME OF THE FATHER, THE SON AND THE HOLY GHOST

My Father's Diary

1841 17th June. Received a commission from my old friend, Peter Grant, to enlarge and restore the chancel of his church at Hagarstone, in the wilds of the west country.

5th July. Went down to Hagarstone with my head man, Somers. A very long and tiring journey.

7th July. Got the work well started. The old church is one of special interest to the antiquarian, and I shall endeavour while restoring it to alter the existing arrangements as little as possible. One large tomb, however, must be moved bodily ten feet at least to the southward. Curiously enough there is a somewhat forbidding inscription upon it in Latin, and I am sorry that this particular tomb should have to be moved. It stands amongst the graves of the Kenyons, an old family which has been extinct in these parts for centuries. The inscription on it runs thus:

SARAH 1630

FOR THE SAKE OF THE DEAD AND THE WELFARE OF THE
LIVING, LET THIS SEPULCHRE REMAIN UNTOUCHED
AND ITS OCCUPANT UNDISTURBED UNTIL
THE COMING OF CHRIST.
IN THE NAME OF THE FATHER, THE SON
AND THE HOLY GHOST.

8th July. Took counsel with Grant concerning the 'Sarah Tomb'. We are both very loath to disturb it, but the ground has sunk so beneath it that the safety of the church is in danger; thus we have no choice. However, the work shall be done as reverently as possible under our own direction.

Grant says there is a legend in the neighbourhood that it is the tomb of the last of the Kenyons, the evil Countess Sarah, who was murdered in 1630. She lived quite alone in the old castle, whose ruins still stand three miles from here on the road to Bristol. Her reputation was an evil one even for those days. She was a witch or were-woman, the only companion of her solitude being a familiar in the shape of a huge Asiatic wolf. This creature was reputed to seize upon children, or failing these, sheep and other small animals, and convey them to the castle, where the countess used to suck their blood. It was popularly supposed that she could never be killed. This, however, proved a fallacy, since she was strangled one day by a mad peasant woman who had lost two children, she declaring that they had both been seized and carried off by the countess's familiar. This is a very interesting story, since it points to a local superstition very similar to that of the vampire, existing in Slavonic and Hungarian Europe.

The tomb is built of black marble, surmounted by an enormous slab of the same material. On the slab is a magnificent group of figures. A young and handsome woman reclines upon a couch; round her neck is a piece of rope, the end of which she holds in her hand. At her side is a gigantic dog with bared fangs and lolling tongue. The face of the reclining figure is a cruel one; the corners of the mouth are curiously lifted, showing the sharp points of long canine or dog teeth. The whole group, though magnificently executed, leaves a most unpleasant sensation.

If we move the tomb it will have to be done in two pieces, the covering slab first and then the tomb proper. We have decided to remove the covering slab tomorrow.

9th July. 6 pm. A very strange day.

By noon everything was ready for lifting off the covering stone, and after the men's dinner we started the jacks and pulleys. The slab lifted easily enough, though it fitted closely into its seat and was further secured by some sort of mortar or putty, which must have kept the interior perfectly air-tight.

None of us was prepared for the horrible rush of foul, mouldy air that escaped as the cover lifted clear of its seating. And the contents that gradually came into view were more startling still. There lay the fully dressed body of a woman, wizened and shrunk and ghastly pale as if from starvation. Round her neck was a loose cord, and, judging by the scars still visible, the story of death by strangulation was true enough.

The most horrible part, however, was the extraordinary freshness of the body. Except for the appearance of starvation, life might have been only just extinct. The flesh was soft and white, the eyes were wide open and seemed to stare at us with a fearful understanding in them. The body itself lay on mould, without any pretence to coffin or shell.

For several moments we gazed with horrible curiosity, and then it became too much for my workmen, who implored us to replace the covering slab. That, of course, we would not do; but I set the carpenters to work at once to make a temporary cover while we moved the tomb to its new position. This is a long job, and will take two or three days at least.

9 pm. Just at sunset we were startled by the howling of, seemingly, every dog in the village. It lasted for ten minutes or a quarter of an hour, and then ceased as suddenly as it had begun. This, and a curious mist that has risen round the church, makes me feel rather anxious about the 'Sarah Tomb'. According to the best established traditions of the vampire-haunted countries, the disturbance of dogs or wolves at sunset is supposed to indicate the presence of one of these fiends, and local fog is always considered to be a certain sign. The vampire has the power of producing it for the purpose of concealing its movements near its hiding-place at any time.

I dare not mention or even hint my fears to the rector, for he is, not unnaturally perhaps, a rank disbeliever in many things that I know, from experience, are not only possible but even probable. I must work this out alone at first, and get his aid without his knowing in what direction he is helping me. I shall now watch till midnight at least.

10.15 pm. As I feared and half expected. Just before ten there was another outburst of the hideous howling. It was commenced most distinctly by a particularly horrible and blood-curdling wail from the vicinity of the churchyard. The chorus lasted only a few minutes, however, and at the end of it I saw a large dark shape, like a huge dog, emerge from the fog and lope away at a rapid canter towards the open country. Assuming this to be what I fear, I shall see it return soon after midnight.

12.30 am. I was right. Almost as midnight struck I saw the beast returning. It stopped at the spot where the fog seemed to commence, and, lifting up its head, gave tongue to that particularly horrible long-drawn wail that I had noticed as preceding the outburst earlier in the evening.

Tomorrow I shall tell the rector what I have seen; and if, as I expect, we hear of some neighbouring sheepfold having been raided, I shall get him to watch with me for this nocturnal marauder. I shall also examine the 'Sarah Tomb' for something which he may notice without any previous hint from me.

* * *

10th July. I found the workmen this morning much disturbed in mind about the howling of the dogs. 'We doan't like it, zur,' one of the men said to me, 'we doan't like it; there was summat abroad last night that was unholy.' They were still more uncomfortable when the news came round that a large dog had made a raid upon a flock of sheep, scattering them far and wide, and leaving three of them dead with torn throats in the field.

When I told the rector of what I had seen and what was being said in the village, he immediately decided that we must try and catch or at least identify the beast I had seen. 'Of course,' he said, 'it is some dog lately imported into the neighbourhood, for I know of nothing about here nearly as large as the animal you describe, though its size may be due to the deceptive moonlight.'

This afternoon I asked the rector, as a favour, to assist me in lifting the temporary cover that was on the tomb, giving as an excuse the reason that I wished to obtain a portion of the curious mortar with which it had been sealed. After a slight demur he consented, and we raised the lid. If the sight that met our eyes gave me a shock, at least it appalled Grant.

'Great God!' he exclaimed; 'the woman is alive!' And so it seemed for a moment. The corpse had lost much of its starved appearance and looked hideously fresh and alive. It was still wrinkled and shrunken, but the lips were firm, and of the rich red hue of health. The eyes, if possible, were more appalling than ever, though fixed and staring. At one corner of the mouth I thought I noticed a slight dark-coloured froth, but I said nothing about it then.

'Take your piece of mortar, Harry,' gasped Grant, 'and let us shut the tomb again. God help me! Parson though I am, such dead faces frighten me!'

Nor was I sorry to hide that terrible face again; but I got my bit of mortar, and I have advanced a step towards the solution of the mystery.

This afternoon the tomb was moved several feet towards its new position, but it will be two or three days yet before we shall be ready to replace the slab.

10.15 pm. Again the same howling at sunset, the same fog enveloping the church, and at ten o'clock the same great beast slipping silently out into the open country. I must get the rector's help and watch for its return. But precautions we must take, for if things are as I believe, we take our lives in our hands when we venture out into the night to waylay the – *vampire*. Why not admit it at once? For that the beast I have seen is the vampire of that evil thing in the tomb I can have no reasonable doubt.

Not yet come to its full strength – thank Heaven! – after the starvation of nearly two centuries, for at present it can only maraud as a wolf apparently. But, in a day or two, when full power returns, that dreadful woman in new strength and beauty will be able to leave her refuge. Then it would not be sheep merely that would satisfy her disgusting lust for blood, but victims that would yield their lifeblood without a murmur to her caressing touch – victims that, dying of her foul embrace, themselves must become vampires in their turn to prey on others.

Mercifully my knowledge gives me a safeguard; for that little piece of mortar that I rescued today from the tomb contains a portion of the sacred host, and who holds it, humbly and firmly believing in its virtue, may pass safely through such an ordeal as I intend to submit myself and the rector to tonight.

12.30 am. Our adventure is over for the present, and we are back safe.

After writing the last entry recorded above, I went off to find Grant and tell him that the marauder was out on the prowl again. 'But, Grant,' I said, 'before we start out tonight I must insist that you will let me conduct this affair in my own way; you must promise to put yourself completely under my orders without asking any questions as to the why and wherefore.'

After a little demur, and some excusable chaff on his part at the serious view I was taking of what he called a 'dog hunt', he gave me his promise. I then told him that we were to watch tonight and try to track the mysterious beast, but not to interfere with it in any way. I think, in spite of his jests, that I impressed him with the fact that there might be, after all, good reason for my precautions.

It was just after eleven when we stepped out into the still night.

Our first move was to try to penetrate the dense fog round the church, but there was something so chilly about it, and a faint smell so disgustingly rank and loathsome, that neither our nerves nor our stomachs were proof against it. Instead, we stationed ourselves in the dark shadow of a yew tree that commanded a good view of the wicket entrance to the churchyard.

At midnight the howling of the dogs began again, and in a few minutes we saw a large grey shape, with green eyes shining like lamps, shamble swiftly down the path towards us.

The rector started forward, but I laid a firm hand upon his arm and whispered a warning: 'Remember!' Then we both stood very still and watched as the great beast cantered swiftly by. It was real enough, for we could hear the clicking of its nails on the stone flags. It passed within a few yards of us, and seemed to be nothing more nor less than a great grey wolf, thin and gaunt, with bristling hair and dripping jaws. It stopped where the ˙mist commenced, and turned round. It was truly a horrible sight, and made one's blood run cold. The eyes burned like fires, the upper lip was snarling and raised, showing the great canine teeth, while round the mouth clung and dripped a dark-coloured froth.

It raised its head and gave tongue to its long wailing howl, which was answered from afar by the village dogs. After standing for a few moments it turned and disappeared into the thickest part of the fog.

Very shortly afterwards the atmosphere began to clear, and within ten minutes the mist was all gone, the dogs in the village were silent, and the night seemed to reassume its normal aspect. We examined the spot where the beast had been standing and found, plainly enough upon the stone flags, dark spots of froth and saliva.

'Well, rector,' I said, 'will you admit now, in view of the things you have seen today, in consideration of the legend, the woman in the tomb, the fog, the howling dogs, and, last but not least, the mysterious beast you have seen so close, that there is something not quite normal in it all? Will you put yourself unreservedly in my hands and help me, *whatever I may do*, first to make assurance doubly sure, and finally to take the necessary steps for putting an end to this horror of the night?' I saw that the uncanny influence of the night was strong upon him, and wished to impress it as much as possible.

'Needs must,' he replied, 'when the Devil drives; and in the face of what I have seen I must believe that some unholy forces are at work. Yet, how can they work in the sacred precincts of a church? Shall we not call rather upon Heaven to assist us in our need?'

'Grant,' I said solemnly, 'that we must do, each in his own way. God helps those who help themselves, and by His help and the light of my knowledge we must fight this battle for Him and the poor lost soul within.'

We then returned to the rectory and to our rooms, though I have sat up to write this account while the scene is fresh in my mind.

11th July. Found the workmen again very much disturbed in their minds, and full of a strange dog that had been seen during the night by several people, who had hunted it. Farmer Stotman, who had been watching his sheep (the same flock that had been raided the night before), had surprised it over a fresh carcass and tried to drive it off, but its size and fierceness so alarmed him that he had beaten a hasty retreat for a gun. When he returned the animal was gone, though he found that three more sheep from his flock were dead and torn.

The 'Sarah Tomb' was moved today to its new position; but it was a long, heavy business, and there was not time to replace the covering slab. For this I was glad as in the prosaic light of day the rector almost disbelieves the events of the night, and is prepared to think everything to have been magnified and distorted by our imagination.

As, however, I could not possibly proceed with my war of extermination against this foul thing without assistance, and as there is nobody else I can rely upon, I appealed to him for one more night – to convince him that it was no delusion, but a ghastly, horrible truth, which must be fought and conquered for our own sakes, as well as that of all those living in the neighbourhood.

'Put yourself in my hands, rector,' I said, 'for tonight at least. Let us take those precautions which my study of the subject tells me are the right ones. Tonight you and I must watch in the church; and I feel assured that tomorrow you will be as convinced as I am, and be equally prepared to take those awful steps which I know to be proper, and I must warn you that we shall find a more startling change in the body lying there than you noticed yesterday.'

My words came true; for on raising the wooden cover once more the rank stench of a slaughterhouse arose, making us feel positively sick. There lay the vampire, but how changed from the starved and shrunken corpse we saw two days ago for the first time! The wrinkles had almost disappeared, the flesh was firm and full, the crimson lips grinned horribly over the long pointed teeth, and a distinct smear of blood had trickled down one corner of the mouth. We set our teeth, however, and hardened our hearts. Then we replaced the cover and put what we had collected into a safe place in the vestry. Yet even now Grant could not believe that there was any real or pressing danger concealed in that awful tomb, as he raised strenuous objections to any apparent desecration of the body without further proof. This he shall have tonight. God grant that I am not taking too much on myself! If there is any truth in old legends it would be easy enough to destroy the vampire now; but Grant will not have it.

I hope for the best of this night's work, but the danger in waiting is very great.

6 pm. I have prepared everything: the sharp knives, the pointed stake, fresh garlic, and the wild dog-roses. All these I have taken and concealed in the vestry, where we can get at them when our solemn vigil commences.

If either or both of us die with our fearful task undone, let those reading my record see that this is done. I lay it upon them as a solemn obligation. 'That the vampire be pierced through the heart with the stake, then let the burial service be read over the poor clay at last released from its doom. Thus shall the vampire cease to be, and a lost soul rest.'

12th July. All is over. After the most terrible night of watching and horror, one vampire at least will trouble the world no more. But how thankful should we be to a merciful Providence that that awful tomb was not disturbed by anyone not having the knowledge necessary to deal with its dreadful occupant! I write this with no feelings of self-complacency, but simply with a great gratitude for the years of study I have been able to devote to this subject.

And now to my tale.

Just before sunset last night the rector and I locked ourselves into the church, and took up our position in the pulpit. It was one of those pulpits, to be found in some churches, which is entered from the vestry, the preacher appearing at a good height through an arched opening in the wall. This gave us a sense of security, which we felt we needed, a good view of the interior, and direct access to the implements which I had concealed in the vestry.

The sun set and the twilight gradually deepened and faded. There was, so far, no sign of the usual fog, nor any howling of the dogs. At nine o'clock the moon rose, and her pale light gradually flooded the aisles, and still no sign of any kind from the 'Sarah Tomb'. The rector had asked me several times what he might expect, but I was determined that no words or thought of mine should influence him, and that he should be convinced by his own senses alone.

By half-past ten we were both getting very tired, and I began to think that perhaps after all we should see nothing that night. However, soon after eleven we observed a light mist rising from the 'Sarah Tomb'. It seemed to scintillate and sparkle as it rose, and curled in a sort of pillar or spiral.

I said nothing, but I heard the rector give a sort of gasp as he clutched my arm feverishly. 'Great Heaven!' he whispered, 'it is taking shape.'

And, true enough, in a very few moments we saw standing erect by the tomb the ghastly figure of the Countess Sarah!

She looked thin and haggard still, and her face was deadly white; but the crimson lips looked like a hideous gash in the pale cheeks, and her eyes glared like red coals in the gloom of the church.

It was a fearful thing to watch as she stepped unsteadily down the aisle, staggering a little as if from weakness and exhaustion. This was perhaps natural, as her body must have suffered much physically from her long incarceration, in spite of the unholy forces which kept it fresh and well.

We watched her to the door, and wondered what would happen; but it appeared to present no difficulty, for she melted through it and disappeared.

'Now, Grant,' I said, 'do you believe?'

'Yes,' he replied, 'I must. Everything is in your hands, and I will obey your commands to the letter, if you can only instruct me how to rid my poor people of this unnameable terror.'

'By God's help I will,' said I; 'but you shall be yet more convinced first, for we have a terrible work to do, and much to answer for in the future, before we leave the church again this morning. And now to work, for in its present weak state the vampire will not wander far, but may return at any time, and must not find us unprepared.'

We stepped down from the pulpit, and taking dog-roses and garlic from the vestry, proceeded to the tomb. I arrived first and, throwing off the wooden cover cried: 'Look! It's empty!' There was nothing there! Nothing except the impress of the body in the loose damp mould!

I took the flowers and laid them in a circle round the tomb, for legend teaches us that vampires will not pass over these particular blossoms if they can avoid it.

Then, eight or ten feet away, I made a circle on the stone pavement, large enough for the rector and myself to stand in, and within the circle I placed the implements that I had brought into the church with me.

'Now,' I said, 'from this circle, which nothing unholy can step across, you shall see the vampire face to face, and see her afraid to cross that other circle of garlic and dog-roses to regain her unholy refuge. But on no account step beyond the holy place you stand in, for the vampire has a fearful strength not her own, and, like a snake, can draw her victim willingly to his own destruction.'

Now so far my work was done, and, calling the rector, we stepped into the holy circle to await the vampire's return.

Nor was this long delayed. Presently a damp, cold odour seemed to pervade the church, which made our hair bristle and flesh creep. And then, down the aisle with noiseless feet, came That which we watched for.

I heard the rector mutter a prayer, and I held him tightly by the arm, for he was shivering violently.

Long before we could distinguish the features we saw the glowing eyes and the crimson sensual mouth. She went straight to her tomb, but stopped short when she encountered my flowers. She walked right round the tomb seeking a place to enter, and as she walked she saw us. A spasm of diabolical hate and fury passed over her face; but it quickly vanished, and a smile of love, more devilish still, took its place. She stretched out her arms towards us. Then we saw that round her mouth gathered a bloody froth, and from under her lips long pointed teeth gleamed and champed.

She spoke: a soft soothing voice, a voice that carried a spell with it, and affected us both strangely, particularly the rector. I wished to test as far as possible, without endangering our lives, the vampire's power.

Her voice had a soporific effect, which I resisted easily enough, but which seemed to throw the rector into a sort of trance. More than this: it seemed to compel him to her in spite of his efforts to resist.

'Come!' she said, 'come! I give sleep and peace – sleep and peace – sleep and peace.'

She advanced a little towards us; but not far, for I noted that the sacred circle seemed to keep her back like an iron hand.

My companion seemed to become demoralised and spellbound. He tried to step forward and, finding me detain him, whispered: 'Harry, let go! I must go! She is calling me! I must! I must! Oh, help me! Help me!' And he began to struggle.

It was time to finish.

'Grant!' I cried, in a loud, firm voice, 'in the name of all that you hold sacred, have done and play the man!' He shuddered violently and gasped: 'Where am I?' Then he remembered, and clung to me convulsively for a moment.

At this a look of damnable hate changed the smiling face before us, and with a sort of shriek she staggered back.

'Back!' I cried. 'Back to your unholy tomb! No longer shall you molest the suffering world! Your end is near.'

It was fear that now showed itself in her beautiful face (for it was beautiful in spite of its horror) as she shrank back, back and over the circlet of flowers, shivering as she did so. At last, with a low mournful cry, she appeared to melt back again into her tomb.

As she did so the first gleams of the rising sun lit up the world, and I knew all danger was over for the day.

Taking Grant by the arm, I drew him with me out of the circle and led him to the tomb. There lay the vampire once more, still in her living death as we had a moment before seen her in her devilish life. But in the eyes remained that awful expression of hate, and cringing, appalling fear.

Grant was pulling himself together.

'Now,' I said, 'will you dare the last terrible act and rid the world forever of this horror?'

'By God!' he said solemnly, 'I will. Tell me what to do.'

'Help me lift her out of her tomb. She can harm us no more,' I replied.

With averted faces we set to our terrible task, and laid her out upon the flags.

'Now,' I said, 'read the burial service over the poor body, and then let us give it its release from this living hell that holds it.'

Reverently the rector read the beautiful words, and reverently I made the necessary responses. When it was over I took the stake and, without giving myself time to think, plunged it with all my strength through the heart.

As though really alive, the body for a moment writhed and kicked convulsively, and an awful heart-rending shriek rang through the silent church; then all was still.

Then we lifted the poor body back; and, thank God! the consolation that legend tells is never denied to those who have to do such awful work as ours came at last. Over the face stole a great and solemn peace; the lips lost their crimson hue, the prominent sharp teeth sank back into the mouth, and for a moment we saw before us the calm, pale face of a most beautiful woman, who smiled as she slept. A few minutes more, and she faded away to dust before our eyes as we watched. We set to work and cleaned up every trace of our work, and then departed for the rectory. Most thankful were we to step out of the church, with its horrible associations, into the rosy warmth of the summer morning.

With the above end the notes in my father's diary, though a few days later this further entry occurs:

* * *

15th July. Since the 12th everything has been quiet and as usual. We replaced and sealed up the 'Sarah Tomb' this morning. The workmen were surprised to find the body had disappeared, but took it to be the natural result of exposing it to the air.

One odd thing came to my ears today. It appears that the child of one of the villagers strayed from home the night of the 11th inst., and was found asleep in a coppice near the church, very pale and quite exhausted. There were two small marks on her throat, which have since disappeared.

What does this mean? I have, however, kept it to myself, as, now the vampire is no more, no further danger either to that child or to any other is to be apprehended. It is only those who die of the vampire's embrace that become vampires at death in their turn.

Interview with the Vampire (extract)
Anne Rice

'I see . . .' said the vampire thoughtfully, and slowly he walked across the room towards the window. For a long time he stood there against the dim light from Divisadero Street and the passing beams of traffic. The boy could see the furnishings of the room more clearly now, the round oak table, the chairs. A wash basin hung on one wall with a mirror. He set his briefcase on the table and waited.

'But how much tape do you have with you?' asked the vampire, turning now so the boy could see his profile. 'Enough for the story of a life?'

'Sure, if it's a good life. Sometimes I interview as many as three or four people a night if I'm lucky. But it has to be a good story. That's only fair, isn't it?'

'Admirably fair,' the vampire answered. 'I would like to tell you the story of my life, then. I would like to do that very much.'

'Great,' said the boy. And quickly he removed the small tape recorder from his briefcase, making a check of the cassette and the batteries. 'I'm really anxious to hear why you believe this, why you . . .'

'No,' said the vampire abruptly. 'We can't begin that way. Is your equipment ready?'

'Yes,' said the boy.

'Then sit down. I'm going to turn on the overhead light.'

'But I thought vampires didn't like light,' said the boy. 'If you think the dark adds to the atmosphere . . .' But then he stopped. The vampire was watching him with his back to the window. The boy could make out nothing of his face now, and something about the still figure there distracted him. He started to say something again but he said nothing. And then he sighed with relief when the vampire moved towards the table and reached for the overhead cord.

At once the room was flooded with a harsh yellow light. And the boy, staring up at the vampire, could not repress a gasp. His fingers danced backwards on the table to grasp the edge. 'Dear God!' he whispered, and then he gazed, speechless, at the vampire.

The vampire was utterly white and smooth, as if he were sculpted from bleached bone, and his face was as seemingly inanimate as a statue, except for two brilliant green eyes that looked down at the boy intently like flames in a skull. But then the vampire smiled almost wistfully, and the smooth white substance of his face moved with the infinitely flexible but minimal lines of a cartoon. 'Do you see?' he asked softly.

The boy shuddered, lifting his hand as if to shield himself from a powerful light. His eyes moved slowly over the finely tailored black coat he'd only glimpsed in the bar, the long folds of the cape, the black silk tie knotted at the throat, and the gleam of the white collar that was as white as the vampire's flesh. He stared at the vampire's full black hair, the waves that were combed back over the tips of the ears, the curls that barely touched the edge of the white collar.

'Now, do you still want the interview?' the vampire asked.

The boy's mouth was open before the sound came out. He was nodding. Then he said, 'Yes.'

The vampire sat down slowly opposite him and, leaning forward, said gently, confidentially, 'Don't be afraid. Just start the tape.'

And then he reached out over the length of the table. The boy recoiled, sweat running down the sides of his face. The vampire clamped a hand on the boy's shoulder and said, 'Believe me, I won't hurt you. I want this opportunity. It's more important to me than you can realize now. I want you to begin.' And he withdrew his hand and sat collected, waiting.

It took a moment for the boy to wipe his forehead and his lips with a handkerchief, to stammer that the microphone was in the machine, to press the button, to say that the machine was on.

'You weren't always a vampire, were you?' he began.

'No,' answered the vampire. 'I was a twenty-five-year-old man when I became a vampire, and the year was 1791.'

The boy was startled by the preciseness of the date and he repeated it before he asked, 'How did it come about?'

'There's a simple answer to that. I don't believe I want to give simple answers,' said the vampire. 'I think I want to tell the real story . . .'

'Yes,' the boy said quickly. He was folding his handkerchief over and over and wiping his lips now with it again.

'There was a tragedy . . .' the vampire started. 'It was my younger brother . . . He died.' And then he stopped, so that the boy cleared his throat and wiped at his face again before stuffing the handkerchief almost impatiently into his pocket.

'It's not painful, is it?' he asked timidly.

'Does it seem so?' asked the vampire. 'No.' He shook his head. 'It's simply that I've only told this story to one other person. And that was so long ago. No, it's not painful . . .'

'We were living in Louisiana then. We'd received a land grant and settled two indigo plantations on the Mississippi very near New Orleans . . .'

'Ah, that's the accent . . .' the boy said softly.

For a moment the vampire stared blankly. 'I have an accent?' He began to laugh.

And the boy, flustered, answered quickly. 'I noticed it in the bar when I asked you what you did for a living. It's just a slight sharpness to the consonants, that's all. I never guessed it was French.'

'It's all right,' the vampire assured him. 'I'm not as shocked as I pretend to be. It's only that I forget it from time to time. But let me go on . . .'

'Please . . .' said the boy.

'I was talking about the plantations. They had a great deal to do with it, really, my becoming a vampire. But I'll come to that. Our life there was both luxurious and primitive. And we ourselves found it extremely attractive. You see, we lived far better there than we could have ever lived in France. Perhaps the sheer wilderness of Louisiana only made it seem so, but seeming so, it was. I remember the imported furniture that cluttered the house.' The vampire smiled. 'And the harpsichord; that was lovely. My sister used to play it. On summer evenings, she would sit at the keys with her back to the open french windows. And I can still remember that thin, rapid music and the vision of the swamp rising beyond her, the moss-hung cypresses floating against the sky. And there were the sounds of the swamp, a chorus of creatures, the cry of the birds. I think we loved it. It made the rosewood furniture all the more precious, the music more delicate and desirable. Even when the wisteria tore the shutters off the attic windows and worked its tendrils right into the whitewashed brick in less than a year . . . Yes, we loved it. All except my brother. I don't think I ever heard him complain of anything, but I knew how he felt. My father was dead then, and I was head of the family and I had to defend him constantly from my mother and sister. They wanted to take him visiting, and to New Orleans for parties, but he hated these things. I think he stopped going altogether before he was twelve. Prayer was what mattered to him, prayer and his leather-bound lives of the saints.

'Finally I built him an oratory removed from the house, and he began to spend most of every day there and often the early evening. It was ironic, really. He was so different from us, so different from everyone, and I was so regular! There was nothing extraordinary about me whatsoever.' The vampire smiled.

'Sometimes in the evening I would go out to him and find him in the garden near the oratory, sitting absolutely composed on a stone bench there, and I'd tell him my troubles, the difficulties I had with the slaves, how I distrusted the overseer or the weather or my brokers . . . all the problems that made up the length and breadth of my existence. And he would listen, making only a few comments, always sympathetic, so that when I left him I had the distinct impression he had solved everything for me. I didn't think I could deny him anything, and I vowed that no matter how it would break my heart to lose him, he could enter the priesthood when the time came. Of course, I was wrong.' The vampire stopped.

For a moment the boy only gazed at him and then he started as if awakened from deep thought, and he floundered, as if he could not find the right words. 'Ah . . . he didn't want to be a priest?' the boy asked. The vampire studied him as if trying to discern the meaning of his expression. Then he said:

'I meant that I was wrong about myself, about my not denying him anything.' His eyes moved over the far wall and fixed on the panes of the window. 'He began to see visions.'

'Real visions?' the boy asked, but again there was hesitation, as if he were thinking of something else.

'I didn't think so,' the vampire answered. 'It happened when he was fifteen. He was very handsome then. He had the smoothest skin and the largest blue eyes. He was robust, not thin as I am now and was then . . . but his eyes . . . it was as if when I looked into his eyes I was standing alone on the edge of the world . . . on a windswept ocean beach. There was nothing but the soft roar of the waves. Well,' he said, his eyes still fixed on the window panes, 'he began to see visions. He only hinted at this at first, and he stopped taking his meals altogether. He lived in the oratory. At any hour of day or night, I could find him on the bare flagstones kneeling before the altar. And the oratory itself was neglected. He stopped tending the candles or changing the altar cloths or even sweeping out the leaves. One night I became really alarmed when I stood in the rose arbour watching him for one solid hour, during which he never moved from his knees and never once lowered his arms, which he held outstretched in the form of a cross. The slaves all thought he was mad.' The vampire raised his eyebrows in wonder. 'I was convinced that he was only . . . overzealous. That in his love for God, he had perhaps gone too far. Then he told me about the visions. Both St Dominic and the Blessed Virgin Mary had come to him in the oratory. They had told him he was to sell all our property in Louisiana, everything we owned, and use the money to do God's work in France. My brother was to be a great religious leader, to return the country to its former fervor, to turn the tide against atheism and the Revolution. Of course, he had no money of his own. I was to sell the plantations and our town houses in New Orleans and give the money to him.'

Again the vampire stopped. And the boy sat motionless regarding him, astonished. 'Ah . . . excuse me,' he whispered. 'What did you say? Did you sell the plantations?'

'No,' said the vampire, his face calm as it had been from the start. 'I laughed at him. And he . . . he became incensed. He insisted his command came from the Virgin herself. Who was I to disregard it? Who indeed?' he asked softly, as if he were thinking of this again. 'Who indeed? And the more he tried to convince me, the more I laughed. It was nonsense, I told him, the product of an immature and even morbid mind. The oratory was a mistake, I said to him; I would have it torn down at once. He would go to school in New Orleans and get such inane notions out of his head. I don't remember all that I said. But I remember the feeling. Behind all this contemptuous dismissal on my part was a smouldering anger and a disappointment. I was bitterly disappointed. I didn't believe him at all.'

'But that's understandable,' said the boy quickly when the vampire paused, his expression of astonishment softening. 'I mean, would anyone have believed him?'

'Is it so understandable?' The vampire looked at the boy. 'I think perhaps it was vicious egotism. Let me explain. I loved my brother, as I told you, and at times I believed him to be a living saint. I encouraged him in his prayer and meditations, as I said, and I was willing to give him up to the priesthood. And if someone had told me of a saint in Arles or Lourdes who saw visions, I would have believed it. I was a Catholic; I believed in saints. I lit tapers before their marble statues in churches; I knew their pictures, their symbols, their names. But I didn't, couldn't believe my brother. Not only did I not believe he saw visions, I couldn't entertain the notion for a moment. Now, why? Because he was my brother. Holy he might be, peculiar most definitely; but Francis of Assisi, no. Not my brother. No brother of mine could be such. That is egotism. Do you see?'

The boy thought about it before he answered and then he nodded and said that yes, he thought that he did.

'Perhaps he saw the visions,' said the vampire.

'Then you . . . you don't claim to know . . . now . . . whether he did or not?'

'No, but I do know that he never wavered in his conviction for a second. That I know now and knew then the night he left my room crazed and grieved. He never wavered for an instant. And within minutes, he was dead.'

'How?' the boy asked.

'He simply walked out of the french doors on to the gallery and stood for a moment at the head of the brick stairs. And then he fell. He was dead when I reached the bottom, his neck broken.' The vampire shook his head in consternation, but his face was still serene.

'Did you see him fall?' asked the boy. 'Did he lose his footing?'

'No, but two of the servants saw it happen. They said that he had looked up as if he had just seen something in the air. Then his entire body moved forward as if being swept by a wind. One of them said he was about to say something when he fell. I thought that he was about to say something too, but it was at that moment I turned away from the window. My back was turned when I heard the noise.' He glanced at the tape recorder. 'I could not forgive myself. I felt responsible for his death,' he said. 'And everyone else seemed to think I was responsible also.'

'But how could they? You said they saw him fall.'

'It wasn't a direct accusation. They simply knew that something had passed between us that was unpleasant. That we had argued minutes before the fall. The servants had heard us, my mother had heard us. My mother would not stop asking me what had happened and why my brother, who was so quiet, had been shouting. Then my sister joined in, and of course I refused to say. I was so bitterly shocked and miserable that I had no patience with anyone, only the vague determination they would not know about his "visions". They would not know that he had become, finally, not a saint, but only a . . . fanatic. My sister went to bed rather than face the funeral, and my mother told everyone in the parish that something horrible had happened in my room which I would not reveal; and even the police questioned me, on the word of my own mother. Finally the priest came to see me and demanded to know what had gone on. I told no one. It was only a discussion, I said. I was not on the gallery when he fell, I protested, and they all stared at me as if I'd killed him. And I felt that I'd killed him. I sat in the parlour beside his coffin for two days thinking, I have killed him. I stared at his face until spots appeared before my eyes and I nearly fainted. The back of his skull had been shattered on the pavement, and his head had the wrong shape on the pillow. I forced myself to stare at it, to study it simply because I could hardly endure the pain and the smell of decay, and I was tempted over and over to try to open his eyes. All these were mad thoughts, mad impulses. The main thought was this: I had laughed at him; I had not believed him; I had not been kind to him. He had fallen because of me.'

'This really happened, didn't it?' the boy whispered. 'You're telling me something . . . that's true.'

'Yes,' said the vampire, looking at him without surprise. 'I want to go on telling you.' But as his eyes passed over the boy and returned to the window, he showed only faint interest in the boy, who seemed engaged in some silent inner struggle.

'But you said you didn't know about the visions, that you, a vampire . . . didn't know for certain whether . . .'

'I want to take things in order,' said the vampire, 'I want to go on telling you things as they happened. No, I don't know about the visions. To this day.' And again he waited until the boy said:

'Yes, please, please go on.'

'Well, I wanted to sell the plantations. I never wanted to see the house or the oratory again. I leased them finally to an agency which would work them for me and manage things so I need never go there, and I moved my mother and sister to one of the town houses in New Orleans. Of course, I did not escape my brother for a moment. I could think of nothing but his body rotting in the ground. He was buried in the St Louis cemetery in New Orleans, and I did everything to avoid passing those gates; but still I thought of him constantly. Drunk or sober, I saw his body rotting in the coffin, and I couldn't bear it. Over and over I dreamed that he was at the head of the steps and I was holding his arm, talking kindly to him, urging him back into the bedroom, telling him gently that I did believe him, that he must pray for me to have faith. Meantime, the slaves on Pointe du Lac (that was my plantation) had begun to talk of seeing his ghost on the gallery, and the overseer couldn't keep order. People in society asked my sister offensive questions about the whole incident, and she became an hysteric. She wasn't really an hysteric. She simply thought she ought to react that way, so she did. I drank all the time and was at home as little as possible. I lived like a man who wanted to die but who had no courage to do it himself. I walked black streets and alleys alone; I passed out in cabarets. I backed out of two duels more from apathy than cowardice and truly wished to be murdered. And then I was attacked. It might have been anyone – and my invitation was open to sailors, thieves, maniacs, anyone. But it was a vampire. He caught me just a few steps from my door one night and left me for dead, or so I thought.'

'You mean . . . he sucked your blood?' the boy asked.

'Yes,' the vampire laughed. 'He sucked my blood. That is the way it's done.'

'But you lived,' said the young man. 'You said he left you for dead.'

'Well, he drained me almost to the point of death, which was for him sufficient. I was put to bed as soon as

I was found, confused and really unaware of what had happened to me. I suppose I thought that drink had finally caused a stroke. I expected to die now and had no interest in eating or drinking or talking to the doctor. My mother sent for the priest. I was feverish by then and I told the priest everything, all about my brother's visions and what I had done. I remember I clung to his arm, making him swear over and over he would tell no one. "I know I didn't kill him," I said to the priest finally. "It's that I cannot live now that he's dead. Not after the way I treated him."

'"That's ridiculous," he answered me. "Of course you can live. There's nothing wrong with you but self-indulgence. Your mother needs you, not to mention your sister. And as for this brother of yours, he was possessed of the devil." I was so stunned when he said this I couldn't protest. The devil made the visions, he went on to explain. The devil was rampant. The entire country of France was under the influence of the devil, and the Revolution had been his greatest triumph. Nothing would have saved my brother but exorcism, prayer, and fasting, men to hold him down while the devil raged in his body and tried to throw him about. "The devil threw him down the steps; it's perfectly obvious," he declared. "You weren't talking to your brother in that room, you were talking to the devil." Well, this enraged me. I believed before that I had been pushed to my limits, but I had not. He went on talking about the devil, about voodoo amongst the slaves and cases of possession in other parts of the world. And I went wild. I wrecked the room in the process of nearly killing him.'

'But your strength . . . the vampire . . .?' asked the boy.

'I was out of my mind,' the vampire explained. 'I did things I could not have done in perfect health. The scene is confused, pale, fantastical now. But I do remember that

I drove him out of the back doors of the house, across the courtyard, and against the brick wall of the kitchen, where I pounded his head until I nearly killed him. When I was subdued finally, and exhausted then almost to the point of death, they bled me. The fools. But I was going to say something else. It was then that I conceived of my own egotism. Perhaps I'd seen it reflected in the priest. His contemptuous attitude toward my brother reflected my own; his immediate and shallow carping about the devil; his refusal to even entertain the idea that sanctity had passed so close.'

'But he did believe in possession by the devil.'

'That is a much more mundane idea,' said the vampire immediately. 'People who cease to believe in God or goodness altogether still believe in the devil. I don't know why. No, I do indeed know why. Evil is always possible. And goodness is eternally difficult. But you must understand, possession is really another way of saying someone is mad. I felt it was, for the priest. I'm sure he'd seen madness. Perhaps he had stood right over raving madness and pronounced it possession. You don't have to see Satan when he is exorcised. But to stand in the presence of a saint . . . To believe that the saint has seen a vision. No, it's egotism, our refusal to believe it could occur in our midst.'

'I never thought of it in that way,' said the boy. 'But what happened to you? You said they bled you to cure you, and that must have nearly killed you.'

The vampire laughed. 'Yes. It certainly did. But the vampire came back that night. You see, he wanted Pointe du Lac, my plantation.

'It was very late, after my sister had fallen asleep. I can remember it as if it were yesterday. He came in from the courtyard, opening the french doors without a sound, a tall fair-skinned man with a mass of blond hair and a graceful, almost feline quality to his movements. And gently, he draped a shawl over my sister's eyes and lowered the wick of the lamp. She dozed there beside the basin and the cloth with which she'd bathed my forehead, and she never once stirred under that shawl until morning. But by that time I was greatly changed.'

'What was this change?' asked the boy.

The vampire sighed. He leaned back against the chair and looked at the walls.

'At first I thought he was another doctor, or someone summoned by the family to try to reason with me. But this suspicion was removed at once. He stepped close to my bed and leaned down so that his face was in the lamplight, and I saw that he was no ordinary man at all. His gray eyes burned with an incandescence, and the long white hands which hung by his sides were not those of a human being. I think I knew everything in that instant, and all that he told me was only aftermath. What I mean is, the moment I saw him, saw his extraordinary aura and knew him to be no creature I'd ever known, I was reduced to nothing. That ego which could not accept the presence of an extraordinary human being in its midst was crushed. All my conceptions, even my guilt and wish to die, seemed utterly unimportant. I completely forgot myself!' he said, now silently touching his breast with his fist. 'I forgot myself totally. And in the same instant knew totally the meaning of possibility. From then on I experienced only increasing wonder. As he talked to me and told me of what I might become, of what his life had been and stood to be, my past shrank to embers. I saw my life as if I stood apart from it, the vanity, the self-serving, the constant fleeing from one petty annoyance after another, the lip service to God and the Virgin and a host of saints whose names filled my prayer books, none of whom made the slightest difference in a narrow, materialistic, and selfish existence. I saw my real gods . . . the gods of most men. Food, drink, and security in conformity. Cinders.'

The boy's face was tense with a mixture of confusion and amazement. 'And so you decided to become a vampire?' he asked. The vampire was silent for a moment.

'Decided. It doesn't seem the right word. Yet I cannot say it was inevitable from the moment that he stepped into that room. No, indeed, it was not inevitable. Yet I can't say I decided. Let me say that when he'd finished speaking, no other decision was possible for me, and I pursued my course without a backward glance. Except for one.'

'Except for one? What?'

'My last sunrise,' said the vampire. 'That morning, I was not yet a vampire. And I saw my last sunrise.

'I remember it completely; yet I do not think I remember any other sunrise before it. I remember the light came first to the tops of the french windows, a paling behind the lace curtains, and then a gleam growing brighter and brighter in patches among the leaves of the trees. Finally the sun came through the windows themselves and the lace lay in shadows on the stone floor, and all over the form of my sister, who was still sleeping, shadows of lace on the shawl over her shoulders and head. As soon as she was warm, she pushed the shawl away without awakening, and then the sun shone full on her eyes and she tightened her eyelids. Then it was gleaming on the table where she rested her head on her arms, and gleaming, blazing, in the water in the pitcher. And I could feel it on my hands on the counterpane and then on my face. I lay in the bed thinking about all the things the vampire had told me, and then it was that I said goodbye to the sunrise and went out to become a vampire. It was . . . the last sunrise.'

The vampire was looking out the window again. And when he stopped, the silence was so sudden the boy seemed to hear it. Then he could hear the noises from the street. The sound of a truck was deafening. The light cord stirred with the vibration. Then the truck was gone.

'Do you miss it?' he asked then in a small voice.

'Not really,' said the vampire. 'There are so many other things. But where were we? You want to know how it happened, how I became a vampire.'

'Yes,' said the boy. 'How did you change, exactly?'

'I can't tell you exactly,' said the vampire. 'I can tell you about it, enclose it with words that will make the value of it to me evident to you. But I can't tell you exactly, any more than I could tell you exactly what is the experience of sex if you have never had it.'

The young man seemed struck suddenly with still another question, but before he could speak the vampire went on. 'As I told you, this vampire Lestat wanted the plantation. A mundane reason, surely, for granting me a life which will last until the end of the world; but he was not a very discriminating person. He didn't consider the world's small population of vampires as being a select club, I should say. He had human problems, a blind father who did not know his son was a vampire and must not find out. Living in New Orleans had become too difficult for him, considering his needs and the necessity to care for his father, and he wanted Pointe du Lac.

'We went at once to the plantation the next evening, ensconced the blind father in the master bedroom, and I proceeded to make the change. I cannot say that it consisted in any one step really – though one, of course, was the step beyond which I could make no return. But there were several acts involved, and the first was the death of the overseer. Lestat took him in his sleep. I was to watch and to approve; that is, to witness the taking of a human life as proof of my commitment and part of my change. This proved without doubt the most difficult part for me. I've told you I had no fear regarding my own death, only a squeamishness about taking my life myself. But I had a most high regard for the life of others, and a horror of death most recently developed because of my brother. I had to watch the overseer awake with a start, try to throw off Lestat with both hands, fail, then lie there struggling under Lestat's grasp, and finally go limp, drained of blood. And die. He did not die at once. We stood in his narrow bedroom for the better part of an hour watching him die. Part of my change, as I said. Lestat would never have stayed otherwise. Then it was necessary to get rid of the overseer's body. I was almost sick from this. Weak and feverish already, I had little reserve; and handling the dead body with such a purpose caused me nausea. Lestat was laughing, telling me callously that I would feel so different once I was a vampire that I would laugh, too. He was wrong about that. I never laugh at death, no matter how often and regularly I am the cause of it.

'But let me take things in order. We had to drive up the river road until we came to open fields and leave the overseer there. We tore his coat, stole his money, and saw to it his lips were stained with liquor. I knew his wife, who lived in New Orleans, and knew the state of desperation she would suffer when the body was discovered. But more than sorrow for her, I felt pain that she would never know what had happened, that her husband had not been found drunk on the road by robbers. As we beat the body, bruising the face and the shoulders, I became more and more aroused. Of course, you must realize that all this time the vampire Lestat was extraordinary. He was no more human to me than a biblical angel. But under this pressure, my enchantment with him was strained. I had seen my becoming a vampire in two lights: The first light was simply enchantment; Lestat had overwhelmed me on my deathbed. But the other light was my wish for self-destruction. My desire to be thoroughly damned. This was the open door through which Lestat had come on both the first and second occasion. Now I was not destroying myself but someone else. The overseer, his wife, his family. I recoiled and might have fled from Lestat, my sanity thoroughly shattered, had not he sensed with an infallible instinct what was happening. Infallible instinct . . .' The vampire mused. 'Let me say the powerful instinct of a vampire to whom even the slightest change in a human's facial expression is as apparent as a gesture. Lestat had preternatural timing. He rushed me into the carriage and whipped the horses home. "I want to die," I began to murmur. "This is unbearable. I want to die. You have it in your power to kill me. Let me die." I refused to look at him, to be spellbound by the sheer beauty of his appearance. He spoke my name to me softly, laughing. As I said, he was determined to have the plantation.'

'But would he have let you go?' asked the boy. 'Under any circumstances?'

'I don't know. Knowing Lestat as I do now, I would say he would have killed me rather than let me go. But this was what I wanted, you see. It didn't matter. No, this was what I thought I wanted. As soon as we reached the house, I jumped down out of the carriage and walked, a zombie, to the brick stairs where my brother had fallen. The house had been unoccupied for months now, the overseer having his own cottage, and the Louisiana heat and damp were already picking apart the steps. Every crevice was sprouting grass and even small wildflowers. I remember feeling the moisture which in the night was cool as I sat down on the lower steps and even rested my head against the brick and felt the little wax-stemmed

wildflowers with my hands. I pulled a clump of them out
of the easy dirt in one hand. "I want to die; kill me. Kill
me," I said to the vampire. "Now I am guilty of murder.
I can't live." He sneered with the impatience of people
listening to the obvious lies of others. And then in a flash
he fastened on me just as he had on my man. I thrashed
against him wildly. I dug my boot into his chest and
kicked him as fiercely as I could, his teeth stinging my
throat, the fever pounding in my temples. And with a
movement of his entire body, much too fast for me to see,
he was suddenly standing disdainfully at the foot of the
steps. "I thought you wanted to die, Louis," he said.'

The boy made a soft, abrupt sound when the vampire
said his name which the vampire acknowledged with the
quick statement, 'Yes, that is my name,' and went on.

'Well, I lay there helpless in the face of my own
cowardice and fatuousness again,' he said. 'Perhaps so
directly confronted with it, I might in time have gained
the courage to truly take my life, not to whine and beg for
others to take it. I saw myself turning on a knife then,
languishing in a day-to-day suffering which I found
as necessary as penance from the confessional, truly
hoping death would find me unawares and render
me fit for eternal pardon. And also I saw myself as if in a
vision standing at the head of the stairs, just where my
brother had stood, and then hurtling my body down on
the bricks.

'But there was no time for courage. Or shall I say, there
was no time in Lestat's plan for anything but his plan.
"Now listen to me, Louis," he said, and he lay down
beside me now on the steps, his movement so graceful
and so personal that at once it made me think of a lover.
I recoiled. But he put his right arm around me and pulled
me close to his chest. Never had I been this close to him
before, and in the dim light I could see the magnificent

radiance of his eye and the unnatural mask of his skin. As I tried to move, he pressed his right fingers against my lips and said, "Be still. I am going to drain you now to the very threshold of death, and I want you to be quiet, so quiet that you can almost hear the flow of blood through your veins, so quiet that you can hear the flow of that same blood through mine. It is your consciousness, your will, which must keep you alive." I wanted to struggle, but he pressed so hard with his fingers that he held my entire prone body in check; and as soon as I stopped my abortive attempt at rebellion, he sank his teeth into my neck.'

The boy's eyes grew huge. He had drawn farther and farther back in his chair as the vampire spoke, and now his face was tense, his eyes narrow, as if he were preparing to weather a blow.

'Have you ever lost a great amount of blood?' asked the vampire. 'Do you know the feeling?'

The boy's lips shaped the word *no*, but no sound came out. He cleared his throat. 'No,' he said.

'Candles burned in the upstairs parlour, where we had planned the death of the overseer. An oil lantern swayed in the breeze on the gallery. All of this light coalesced and began to shimmer, as though a golden presence hovered above me, suspended in the stairwell, softly entangled with the railings, curling and contracting like smoke. "Listen, keep your eyes wide," Lestat whispered to me, his lips moving against my neck. I remember that the movement of his lips raised the hair all over my body, sent a shock of sensation through my body that was not unlike the pleasure of passion . . .'

He mused, his right fingers slightly curled beneath his chin, the first finger appearing to lightly stroke it. 'The result was that within minutes I was weak to paralysis. Panic-stricken, I discovered I could not even will myself to speak. Lestat still held me, of course, and his arm was like the weight of an iron bar. I felt his teeth withdraw with such a keenness that the two puncture wounds seemed enormous, lined with pain. And now he bent over my helpless head and, taking his right hand off me, bit his own wrist. The blood flowed down upon my shirt and coat, and he watched it with a narrow, gleaming eye. It seemed an eternity that he watched it, and that shimmer of light now hung behind his head like the backdrop of an apparition. I think that I knew what he meant to do even before he did it, and I was waiting in my helplessness as if I'd been waiting for years. He pressed his bleeding wrist to my mouth, said firmly, a little impatiently. "Louis, drink." And I did. "Steady, Louis," and "Hurry," he whispered to me a number of times. I drank, sucking the blood out of the holes, experiencing for the first time since infancy the special pleasure of sucking nourishment, the body focused with the mind upon one vital source. Then something happened.' The vampire sat back, a slight frown on his face.

'How pathetic it is to describe these things which can't truly be described,' he said, his voice low almost to a whisper. The boy sat as if frozen.

'I saw nothing but that light then as I drew blood. And then this next thing, this next thing was . . . sound. A dull roar at first and then a pounding like the pounding of a drum, growing louder and louder, as if some enormous creature were coming up on one slowly through a dark and alien forest, pounding as he came, a huge drum. And then there came the pounding of another drum, as if another giant were coming yards behind him, and each giant, intent on his own drum, gave no notice to the rhythm of the other. The sound grew louder and louder until it seemed to fill not just my hearing but all my senses, to be throbbing in my lips and fingers, in the flesh of my temples, in my veins. Above all, in my veins, drum and then the other drum; and then Lestat pulled his wrist free suddenly, and I opened my eyes and checked myself in a moment of reaching for his wrist, grabbing it, forcing it back to my mouth at all costs; I checked myself because I realized that the drum was my heart, and the second drum had been his.' The vampire sighed. 'Do you understand?'

The boy began to speak, and then he shook his head. 'No . . . I mean, I do,' he said. 'I mean, I . . .'

'Of course,' said the vampire, looking away.

'Wait, wait!' said the boy in a welter of excitement. 'The tape is almost gone. I have to turn it over.' The vampire watched patiently as he changed it.

'What happened then?' the boy asked. His face was moist, and he wiped it hurriedly with his handkerchief.

'I saw as a vampire,' said the vampire, his voice now slightly detached. It seemed almost distracted. Then he drew himself up. 'Lestat was standing again at the foot of the stairs, and I saw him as I could not possibly have seen him before. He had seemed white to me before, starkly white, so that in the night he was almost luminous; and now I saw him filled with his own life and own blood: he was radiant, not luminous. And then I saw that not only Lestat had changed, but all things had changed.

'It was as if I had only just been able to see colours and shapes for the first time. I was so enthralled with the buttons on Lestat's black coat that I looked at nothing else for a long time. Then Lestat began to laugh, and I heard his laughter as I had never heard anything before. His heart I still heard like the beating of a drum, and now came this metallic laughter. It was confusing, each sound running into the next sound, like the mingling reverberations of bells, until I learned to separate the sounds, and then they overlapped, each soft but distinct, increasing but discrete, peals of laughter.' The vampire smiled with delight. 'Peals of bells.'

'"Stop looking at my buttons," Lestat said. "Go out there into the trees. Rid yourself of all the human waste in your body, and don't fall so madly in love with the night that you lose your way!"

'That, of course, was a wise command. When I saw the moon on the flagstones, I became so enamoured with it that I must have spent an hour there. I passed my brother's oratory without so much as a thought of him, and standing among the cottonwood and oaks, I heard the night as if it were a chorus of whispering women, all beckoning me to their breasts. As for my body, it was not yet totally converted, and as soon as I became the least accustomed to the sounds and sights, it began to ache. All my human fluids were being forced out of me. I was dying as a human, yet completely alive as a vampire; and with my awakened senses, I had to preside over the death of my body with a certain discomfort and then, finally, fear. I ran back up the steps to the parlor, where Lestat was already at work on the plantation papers, going over the expenses and profits for the last year. "You're a rich man," he said to me when I came in. "Something's happening to me," I shouted.

'"You're dying, that's all; don't be a fool. Don't you have any oil lamps? All this money and you can't afford whale oil except for that lantern. Bring me that lantern."

'"Dying!" I shouted. "Dying!"

'"It happens to everyone," he persisted, refusing to help me. As I look back on this, I still despise him for it. Not because I was afraid, but because he might have drawn my attention to these changes with reverence. He might have calmed me and told me I might watch my death with the same fascination with which I had watched and felt the night. But he didn't. Lestat was never the vampire I am.

Not at all.' The vampire did not say this boastfully. He said it as if he would truly have had it otherwise.

'*Alors*,' he sighed. 'I was dying fast, which meant that my capacity for fear was diminishing as rapidly. I simply regret I was not more attentive to the process: Lestat was being a perfect idiot. "Oh, for the love of hell!" he began shouting. "Do you realize I've made no provision for you? What a fool I am." I was tempted to say, "Yes, you are," but I didn't. "You'll have to bed down with me this morning. I haven't prepared you a coffin."'

The vampire laughed. 'The coffin struck such a chord of terror in me I think it absorbed all the capacity for terror I had left. Then came only my mild alarm at having to share a coffin with Lestat. He was in his father's bedroom meantime, telling the old man goodbye, that he would return in the morning. "But where do you go, why must you live by such a schedule!" the old man demanded, and Lestat became impatient. Before this, he'd been gracious to the old man, almost to the point of sickening one, but now he became a bully. "I take care of you, don't I? I've put a better roof over your head than you ever put over mine! If I want to sleep all day and drink all night, I'll do it, damn you!" The old man started to whine. Only my peculiar state of emotions and most unusual feeling of exhaustion kept me from disapproving. I was watching the scene through the open door, enthralled with the colours of the counterpane and the positive riot of colour in the old man's face. His blue veins pulsed beneath his pink and grayish flesh. I found even the yellow of his teeth appealing to me, and I became almost hypnotized by the quivering of his lip. "Such a son, such a son," he said, never suspecting, of course, the true nature of his son. "All right, then, go. I know you keep a woman somewhere; you go to see her as soon as her husband leaves in the morning. Give me my rosary.

What's happened to my rosary?" Lestat said something blasphemous and gave him the rosary . . .'

'But . . .' the boy started.

'Yes?' said the vampire. 'I'm afraid I don't allow you to ask enough questions.'

'I was going to ask, rosaries have crosses on them, don't they?'

'Oh, the rumour about crosses!' the vampire laughed. 'You refer to our being afraid of crosses?'

'Unable to look on them, I thought,' said the boy.

'Nonsense, my friend, sheer nonsense. I can look on anything I like. And I rather like looking on crucifixes in particular.'

'And what about the rumour about keyholes? That you can . . . become steam and go through them.'

'I wish I could,' laughed the vampire. 'How positively delightful. I should like to pass through all manner of different keyholes and feel the tickle of their peculiar shapes. No.' He shook his head. 'That is, how would you say today . . . bullshit?'

The boy laughed despite himself. Then his face grew serious.

'You mustn't be so shy with me,' the vampire said. 'What is it?'

'The story about stakes through the heart,' said the boy, his cheeks colouring slightly.

'The same,' said vampire. 'Bull-shit,' he said, carefully articulating both syllables, so that the boy smiled. 'No magical power whatsoever. Why don't you smoke one of your cigarettes? I see you have them in your shirt pocket.'

'Oh, thank you,' the boy said, as if it were a marvellous suggestion. But once he had the cigarette to his lips, his hands were trembling so badly that he mangled the first fragile book match.

'Allow me,' said the vampire. And, taking the book, he quickly put a lighted match to the boy's cigarette. The boy inhaled, his eyes on the vampire's fingers. Now the vampire withdrew across the table with a soft rustling of garments. 'There's an ashtray on the basin,' he said, and the boy moved nervously to get it. He stared at the few butts in it for a moment, and then, seeing the small waste basket beneath, he emptied the ashtray and quickly set it on the table. His fingers left damp marks on the cigarette when he put it down. 'Is this your room?' he asked.

'No,' answered the vampire. 'Just a room.'

'What happened then?' the boy asked. The vampire appeared to be watching the smoke gather beneath the overhead bulb.

'Ah . . . we went back to New Orleans posthaste,' he said. 'Lestat had his coffin in a miserable room near the ramparts.'

'And you did get into the coffin?'

'I had no choice. I begged Lestat to let me stay in the closet, but he laughed, astonished. "Don't you know what you are?" he asked. "But is it magical? Must it have this shape?" I pleaded. Only to hear him laugh again. I couldn't bear the idea; but as we argued, I realized I had no real fear. It was a strange realization. All my life I'd feared closed places. Born and bred in French houses with lofty ceilings and floor-length windows, I had a dread of being enclosed. I felt uncomfortable even in the confessional in church. It was a normal enough fear. And now I realized as I protested to Lestat, I did not actually feel this anymore. I was simply remembering it. Hanging on to it from habit, from a deficiency of ability to recognize my present and exhilarating freedom. "You're carrying on badly," Lestat said finally. "And it's almost dawn. I should let you die. You will die, you know. The sun will destroy the blood I've given you, in every tissue, every vein. But you shouldn't be feeling this fear at all. I think you're like a man who loses an arm or a leg and keeps insisting that he can feel pain where the arm or leg used to be." Well, that was positively the most intelligent and useful thing Lestat ever said in my presence, and it brought me around at once. "Now, I'm getting into the coffin," he finally said to me in his most disdainful tone, "and you will get in on top of me if you know what's good for you." And I did. I lay face-down on him, utterly confused by my absence of dread and filled with a distaste for being so close to him, handsome and intriguing though he was. And he shut the lid. Then I asked him if I was completely dead. My body was tingling and itching all over. "No, you're not then," he said. "When you are, you'll only hear and see it changing and feel nothing. You should be dead by tonight. Go to sleep."'

'Was he right? Were you . . . dead when you woke up?'

'Yes, changed, I should say. As obviously I am alive. My body was dead. It was some time before it became absolutely cleansed of the fluids and matter it no longer needed, but it was dead. And with the realization of it came another stage in my divorce from human emotions. The first thing which became apparent to me, even while Lestat and I were loading the coffin into a hearse and stealing another coffin from a mortuary, was that I did not like Lestat at all. I was far from being his equal yet, but I was infinitely closer to him than I had been before the death of my body. I can't really make this clear to you for the obvious reason that you are now as I was before my body died. You cannot understand. But before I died, Lestat was absolutely the most overwhelming *experience* I'd ever had. Your cigarette has become one long cylindrical ash.'

'Oh!' The boy quickly ground the filter into the glass. 'You mean that when the gap was closed between you, he lost his . . . spell?' he asked, his eyes quickly fixed on the vampire, his hands now producing a cigarette and match much more easily than before.

'Yes, that's correct,' said the vampire with obvious pleasure. 'The trip back to Pointe du Lac was thrilling. And the constant chatter of Lestat was positively the most boring and disheartening thing I experienced. Of course as I said, I was far from being his equal. I had my dead limbs to contend with . . . to use his comparison. And I learned that on that very night, when I had to make my first kill.'

The vampire reached across the table now and gently brushed an ash from the boy's lapel, and the boy stared at his withdrawing hand in alarm. 'Excuse me,' said the vampire. 'I didn't mean to frighten you.'

'Excuse me,' said the boy. 'I just got the impression suddenly that your arm was . . . abnormally long. You reached so far without moving!'

'No,' said the vampire, resting his hands again on his crossed knees. 'I moved forward much too fast for you to see. It was an illusion.'

'You moved forward? But you didn't. You were sitting just as you are now, with your back against the chair.'

'No,' repeated the vampire firmly. 'I moved forward as I told you. Here, I'll do it again.' And he did it again, and the boy stared with the same mixture of confusion and fear. 'You still didn't see it,' said the vampire. 'But, you see, if you look at my outstretched arm now, it's really not remarkably long at all.' And he raised his arm, first finger pointing heavenward as if he were an angel about to give the Word of the Lord. 'You have experienced a fundamental difference between the way you see and I see. My gesture appeared slow and somewhat languid to me. And the sound of my finger brushing your coat was quite audible. Well, I didn't mean to frighten you,

I confess. But perhaps you can see from this that my return to Pointe du Lac was a feast of new experiences, the mere swaying of a tree branch in the wind a delight.'

'Yes,' said the boy; but he was still visibly shaken. The vampire eyed him for a moment, and then he said, 'I was telling you . . .'

'About your first kill,' said the boy.

Activities

Ghost stories

The Sweeper by A M Burrage

Questions

1 The mystery that begins *The Sweeper* (page 2) is the curious character of Miss Ludgate. Look carefully at the opening section of the story. Then in your own words write a brief paragraph describing what is curious about Miss Ludgate.

2 Look again at this sentence from page 3. 'Yet she was sometimes overwhelmingly generous in her spasmodic charities to individuals, and her kindness to itinerant beggars was proverbial among their fraternity.' What does it mean about Miss Ludgate? Use a dictionary to help you.

3 What do you learn from Tessa's letter (see pages 3–4) about the setting of the story that is in keeping with a traditional ghost story?

4 The atmosphere on pages 7–9 gradually changes to become eerie and frightening, and the writer appeals particularly to descriptions of sound to create horror. Pick out three words or phrases from these pages that show this gradual change.

5 Notice in the description of the Sweeper on pages 11–12 and 13 that Burrage does not need to detail a gory or bloody vision to create a frightening ghost. Pick out three words or phrases from this description that you think make the ghost a frightening vision and explain why you have chosen them.

Activities

The final scene of *The Sweeper* is told very much from the perspectives of Tessa Winyard and Mrs Finch. Using your knowledge of Burrage's writing style (creating ghostly atmosphere by appealing to the senses, particularly sound), rewrite the final scene of the story describing it all from Miss Ludgate's perspective as she hears the Sweeper on the final part of his task and awaits her final moments.

Or

Write a newspaper report on the ghostly happenings at Billington Abbots and Miss Ludgate's final curious death. You will need to include in your report:

- the facts of the story
- opinions and interviews from people involved
- a headline.

The Boys' Toilets by Robert Westall

Questions

1 The first paragraph of *The Boys' Toilets* (see page 18) uses powerful imagery to convey a sense of violence and destruction. Identify any literary devices (for example, similes, personification, metaphors), then explain how each of them works to convey this atmosphere.

2 Why do the girls need to move to a temporary school site?

3 Examine Westall's description of the setting of Harvest Road School on pages 19–20. Pick out three quotations from this description that highlight for you a change of atmosphere in the story to a more eerie setting. Comment on why you think each is effective.

4 In your own words, describe the character of the teacher, Miss Hogg.

5 What happens on page 30 to make Rebeccah begin 'to hate the ghosts in the boys' toilets'?

6 Suspense is an important part of the supernatural genre. Examine the three paragraphs on page 37 where Rebeccah finds the passport and wallet, beginning 'There could be no mistake'. Pick out the verbs that Westall uses to describe her gradual finding of the goods. How does this description create a sense of fear for the reader?

Activities

Imagine you are Rebeccah's father after his visit to Alfred Barnett. Write a letter to the headteacher of the girls' school explaining your understanding of the ghostly happenings at Harvest Road boys' school and the girls' behaviour in 3A. Be careful to keep the tone of the letter friendly but formal, explaining her misjudgement of the girls in a polite but firm manner.

Or

If you enjoyed this story you might like to find out more about Robert Westall and the many books he has written for young people.

Click on www.heineman.co.uk/hotlinks and type in express code 5451P. Our website will link you to a great site about Robert Westall.

Look through the information you are given there and choose another book to read by him.

Fairy tales

Sweet Shop by Marc Alexander

Questions

1 Give yourself five minutes to jot down as many titles of fairy tales as you can remember.

2 Using your list as a reminder, look at the following elements of a story. Which might you generally expect to find in a fairy tale?

- The good stepmother.
- Vampires.
- The wicked stepmother.
- A happy ending.
- Magic and spells.
- Witches or wizards.
- Clear divisions between good and evil.
- Ghosts.
- A depressing ending.
- Martians.
- An ugly prince.
- A handsome prince.
- A clown.
- Talking animals.

Can you think of any other common elements?

3 Examine the first scene of the *Sweet Shop* (pages 57–8), which is set in the classroom. Pick out five quotations from this section that help the reader to think about fairy tales and what they mean to modern life that prepare us for the rest of the story.

4 List the common problems or issues of modern family life that are addressed in this story.

5 Which traditional fairy tale is this story based on? At what point in the story did you realise the parallel?

Activity

Use the sentence starters below to write three paragraphs about *Sweet Shop*, analysing how the writer uses the traditional story to write a modern version. Use quotations to support your answer.

Sweet Shop is a modern fairy story based on
.... about
....

Throughout the story the writer draws many parallels between the modern story and the original traditional version ....

There are also many differences between the traditional version and *Sweet Shop*, which make Marc Alexander's story a thoroughly modern story ....

The Werewolf by Angela Carter

Questions

1 Look carefully at the first two paragraphs of *The Werewolf* (page 67). Using quotations to support your points, comment on:

- what kind of setting the writer describes

- how the length of the sentences reflects this setting

- which adjectives are particularly effective in adding to this setting

- which nouns are particularly effective in adding to this setting.

2 Pick out the words in the first four paragraphs of this story that suggest these people are superstitious and old-fashioned in their lifestyles and beliefs.

3 Pick out any sentences in the story containing words you do not understand. Using a dictionary, explain what you think each sentence means.

4 Pinpoint which line of the story is the first that gives you a clue to the fairy tale that Angela Carter has based this story on? What is the original fairy story?

5 What do we find out about the grandmother near the end of the story?

6 Angela Carter has changed her story to portray a more modern heroine. Pick out three quotations that show this and comment on what they suggest about the girl's character.

Activities

Choose a fairy tale that you know and find a children's version of the tale from school, home, your library or the Internet.

Most children's fairy tales lack detailed description of setting and atmosphere, and rely mostly on plot. Basing your writing on the first few paragraphs of *The Werewolf*, write a new opening to your fairytale for a mature reader. Use appropriate sentences and vocabulary to create a more horrifying and disturbing modern opening to your chosen tale.

You might also like to write a paragraph commenting on your original story and your aims in rewriting the tale, explaining your choices of vocabulary and sentence structure to create setting and atmosphere.

Crime fiction

The Adventure of the Sussex Vampire
by Sir Arthur Conan Doyle

Questions

1   Why does Sherlock Holmes initially dismiss the letter from the solicitors at the beginning of *The Adventure of the Sussex Vampire* (pages 72–4)?

2   Why is Dr Watson surprised when he first sees Mr Ferguson? Use quotations to support your answer.

3   Look at the initial conversation between Holmes and Mr Ferguson on pages 78–9. Their styles of speech are very different. What characteristics of Holmes's language portray him as confident and in control? What characteristics of Ferguson's language convey him as tense and worried? Use quotations to support your answer.

4   Explain in your own words Holmes's explanation of this mystery.

5   Do you think the title of the story is a good one? Give reasons for your answer.

6   Having read the story, what kind of a man and detective is Sherlock Holmes? Pick three words you would use to describe him and support your opinions with quotations from the text.

Activity

Imagine you are planning materials for the exchange visit of a group of American High School students to England. They are interested in studying the great British detective Sherlock Holmes. Research this topic, using both the library and the Internet. Then prepare a leaflet for them giving them information and suggestions about:

A Writer's Cauldron

- visiting Holmes's house in Baker Street
- the biography of Sir Arthur Conan Doyle
- the best Sherlock Holmes stories to read
- other great British detective writers.

You might like to add some sections of your own to the leaflet once you have done your research about the author and his detective.

One place to start might be the web. Click on www.heineman.co.uk/hotlinks and type in express code 5451P. We will link you to a Sherlock Holmes website full of information.

Lamb to the Slaughter by Roald Dahl

Questions

1 Pick out any adjectives from *Lamb to the Slaughter* (page 93) that create a cosy and homely setting for the story in the first paragraph.

2 Reread the first eight paragraphs of the story (see pages 93–4). What does Mary Maloney's behaviour suggest to you about her relationship with her husband? Use quotations to support your answer.

3 What is strange about Mr Maloney's behaviour when he comes home this particular night?

4 What do you think Mr Maloney tells his wife on page 96?

5 In your opinion, which character is shown to be the most calculating and clever in this story?

6 How do these policemen fit in with the usual stereotypes of the perceptive and intelligent heroes of traditional crime fiction?

7 Why do you think Dahl called this story *Lamb to the Slaughter*?

Activity

Imagine that Mrs Maloney was a very different woman from Roald Dahl's creation. Imagine she is a woman who hates her husband and is waiting in anticipation to kill him on his arrival from work that day.

Rewrite the first page of the story (see page 93), keeping the main text the same, but changing any words that you feel need to be made more aggressive, unfriendly and menacing to create a more sinister atmosphere for Mr Maloney's return.

Tip: it might be helpful to underline any words in the original story that create a friendly and cosy atmosphere so that you can see which ones need replacing for your new version.

When you have written your version you might like to read it to someone else in your class and hear their version. Who has most effectively managed to create a sense of evil and menace?

Love stories

The Knight's Tale by Geoffrey Chaucer, retold by Geraldine McCaughrean

Questions

1 A medieval knight would traditionally be expected to be interested in religion, honour, loyalty, love and war. He would have been a very well respected person in society. Find a quotation from *The Knight's Tale* (page 106) for each of the above topics to prove that this story is appropriate to the teller of the tale.

2 Examine the passage on pages 111–12 about the jousting.

   a Pick out three verbs that you think help to create a sense of an exciting fight, then comment on why they work well.

   b Pick out three nouns used during this passage that reflect the equipment of a medieval Knight in battle.

3 Chaucer's tale is interspersed with conversation from the pilgrims who are listening to the tale the Knight is telling them. Which characters are mentioned and what clues can you pick up about their characters?

4 What does Chaucer do at the end of this tale to make you want to read on in the *Canterbury Tales*?

Activity

Look at the following section of *The Knight's Tale*, which is from Chaucer's original written in middle English. This is the section when Palamon first sees Emily.

Using the vocabulary that is given to you, try to write an accurate translation in modern English of Chaucer's original passage. You might like to work with a partner on this exercise. Some of the language might look unfamiliar but try to read any difficult words aloud and see if they sound like a modern English equivalent. Then try to make an intelligent guess using the context of the sentence. Some of the words have been numbered, and their meanings are given on page 229.

Her yellow hair was braided in a tress[1],
Behind her back, a yarde long I guess.
And in the garden at the sun uprist[2]
She walketh up and down where as her list[3].
She gathereth flowers, party[4] white and red,
To make a sotel[5] garland for her head,
And as an angel heavenly she sung.
The greate tower, that was so thick and strong,
Which of the castle was the chief dungeon
Was even joinant[6] to the garden wall,
There as this Emily had her playing.

Bright was the sun, and clear that morrowning,
And Palamon, this woful prisoner,

As was his wont[7], by leave[8] of his gaoler,
Was ris'n, and roamed in a chamber on high,
In which he all the noble city sigh[9],
And eke the garden, full of branches green,
There as this fresh Emelia the sheen
Was in her walk, and roamed up and down.
This sorrowful prisoner, this Palamon
Went in his chamber roaming to and fro,
And to himself complaining of his woe:
That he was born, full oft he said, Alas!
And so befell, by aventure or cas[10],
That through a window thick of many a bar
Of iron great, and square as any spar,
He cast his eyes upon Emelia,
And therewithal he blent[11] and cried, Ah!
As though he stungen[12] were unto the heart.

Vocabulary

[1]tress, plait
[2]sunrise
[3]she wanted
[4]mingled
[5]subtle, well-arranged
[6]adjoining
[7]habit
[8]permission
[9]saw
[10]and so it happened, by chance
[11]started aside
[12]stung, stabbed

Cinderella Girl by Vivien Alcock

Questions

1 What do you learn about the character of Edward's mother from her language and comments in the first two pages (115–16) of *Cinderella Girl*?

2 What do you learn about Michael that suggests he is a little more mature than his friend Edward?

3 Why is Edward attracted to Bella?

4 What is unrequited love (page 119)? If you are unsure, use a dictionary to help you find out.

5 What evidence do you find in the story that suggests one of its main themes is 'growing up'?

Activity

Take a look at the poem below that Edward composes for Meg, saying what he finds attractive about her.

'Your hair is rough and long and needs a cut,
Your mermaid eyes are flecked with gold and green.
Your nose is smudged, your sleeve unravelled but
Of all the girls at school you are my queen.'

Now write a full version of this poem. Look for clues about Meg's personality and appearance throughout the story, then craft your language to put together a poem for her.

Or

Imagine Edward writes to a magazine problem page about his relationship with Bella (outlined in pages 117–19). Write his problem and then the reply from the agony aunt or uncle. What advice do you think Edward should be given? Remember that an agony aunt or uncle would reply in a thoughtful and tactful way.

Gift by Susan Gates

Questions

1 Copy out the similes and metaphors on the first page of *Gift* (page 124) referring to Gift. What does each of them suggest about the narrator's views of him?

2 The narrator's description of the setting from pages 124–6 clearly locate the story in Africa. Pick out three words or phrases that describe the setting, then comment on why you think they convey a sense of Africa.

3 What does the narrator find difficult at first when she is staying with Gift's family?

4 Being romantic can sometimes make a person's judgement unreliable. Pick out two lines in the story that you think reflect the narrator's romantic and misjudged ideas about her relationship with Gift.

5 What suggests that Gift and his intended bride love each other? Use a quotation from the story to support your answer.

Activity

Arranged marriages are a part of many cultures throughout the world. **In a group** discuss what you think might be the benefits and drawbacks of such a system compared to an individual choosing his or her own partner. You might like to research a little about the topic before you start, using your school library, the Internet or by talking to friends and family.

Click on www.heineman.co.uk/hotlinks and type in express code 5451P. Our links will give you a head start on your research.

Science fiction

A Sound of Thunder by Ray Bradbury

Questions

1   Pinpoint the first sentence in *A Sound of Thunder* (page 134) that suggests to you that this story is science fiction.

2   What are Eckels's motives for wanting to go on the safari?

3   Summarise, in your own words, Travis's warning to the men on pages 138–40. How is this issue relevant to our lives today?

4   Look carefully at the description of Tyrannosaurus Rex on pages 142–4. Select three phrases that you think are particularly effective to help you imagine him and comment on the writer's use of language.

5   Discuss with a partner what you think the message of the story is. Write down your conclusions.

Activity

Look at the advertisement below.

> TIME SAFARI, INC.
> SAFARIS TO ANY YEAR IN THE PAST.
> YOU NAME THE ANIMAL.
> WE TAKE YOU THERE.
> YOU SHOOT IT.

Which year in the past would you choose to travel to in response to it? Jot down some possibilities of historical people or events that you would like to see and find out more about.

You will then need to plan a good argument to persuade a group of your classmates that your idea is the one they should choose for a group trip. You will need to research some of the background to your chosen year, using the library or the Internet. Plan the points of your argument, then develop your idea in a presentation to your group as well as listening to their ideas.

Finally, decide through negotiation in your group which idea sounds the most interesting. Remember to think carefully about other people's ideas and how persuasive their arguments are, rather than just insisting that your own idea is the best.

Mind Bend by Martin Martinsen

Questions

1 Which nouns in the first two pages of *Mind Bend* (page 150) immediately suggest to you that this story is within the genre of science fiction? Which are proper nouns and which are common nouns?

2 Pinpoint the simile in the third paragraph of this story. How does it relate to the genre of science fiction?

3 This story is told by a first person narrator and creates a sense of intimacy with the reader. The narrator's style is informal and familiar with the reader. Can you find any examples of this?

4 Technical and futuristic language is a feature of the science fiction genre. What futuristic and technical language can you find in this story?

5 Explain in your own words what the Mindbender's plan was, and how the narrator and his father managed to thwart it.

Activity

Write your own Planet Halfway dictionary for Planet Earth readers of this story. Scan the text of the story for as many unfamiliar technical terms as you can find. Then write them out in alphabetical order and list your own dictionary definitions, using clues from the story and your own imagination.

You might like to add illustrations and a cover to your dictionary. You might also like to look at a standard dictionary to remind yourself of the format and layout of a dictionary page.

Horror stories

The Tomb of Sarah by F G Loring

Questions

1 Why is the narrator's father reluctant to move the tomb at the beginning of the story?

2 What is 'a familiar' (see page 172)?

3 What is horrifying about the appearance of Sarah on page 173?

4 Pick out three words or phrases from the narrator's description of the setting of the story on pages 177–8 that you feel add to the horrifying atmosphere. Comment on how the language appeals to our senses and adds to the sense of horror.

5 The following sentences all come from pages 183–4. Using a dictionary if needed, explain what the bold words mean in the context of their sentences.

- A spasm of **diabolical** hate and fury passed over her face . . .

- Her voice had a **soporific** effect . . .

- My companion seemed to become **demoralised** and **spellbound**.

Activity

Using the details given in *The Tomb of Sarah* write your own instruction manual for anyone who has to deal with vampires.

Think carefully about the formal style and layout necessary for such an instructional document. You might want to add diagrams or pictures to illustrate your instructions.

If you are able to undertake some research into the history and background of vampire superstitions you may also add this as an introduction to your leaflet.

Include a list of 'facts and advice for dealing with vampires' in your manual.

Interview with the Vampire (extract)
by Anne Rice

Questions

1 Part of what is horrifying in *Interview with the Vampire* (page 187) is the fact that the vampire is in control of the interview. Read through the dialogue on the first two pages and note down the evidence you can find to support this.

2 What evidence can you find on the first two pages of this story to suggest that the boy is vulnerable and uneasy?

3 Traditionally vampires are unemotional and inhuman creatures. This vampire is very human and it is horrifying that the author uses this to encourage us to sympathise with him. What evidence can you find on pages 189–93 to suggest that this vampire remains rather human in his actions and emotions when speaking about his past?

4 Look again at page 210. What traditions about vampires does this modern vampire dismiss in this part of the text?

Activity

Imagine you are the boy who interviewed the vampire. A tabloid newspaper has asked you to write an article about finding a real live modern vampire in San Francisco, USA, and your interview with him. It is up to you whether you sensationalise the details from the interview in a way that suggests you believe in the vampire or whether you portray him as a madman with crazy delusions of being a vampire. Remember to think carefully about the style of a tabloid newspaper and include the following elements:

- headline
- subtitles
- pictures
- quotations from the interview
- factual information from the story
- your opinion as the journalist.

Extended writing activities

Compare and contrast the stories *The Adventure of the Sussex Vampire* (page 72) and *Lamb to the Slaughter* (page 93). Plan your essay by writing notes on some of the following aspects of both stories, then use the bullet points to structure your essay. Remember to use quotations from both texts to support your points.

- The characters of the detectives.
- The setting of the stories.
- The way the solutions to the murders are revealed to the readers.
- The murderers in each story and their motives.
- The titles of the stories.
- The language used by the writers in the stories.
- Overall how the writer conforms or manipulates the crime fiction genre.
- Which story you liked best and why.

Examine how the writers of *The Werewolf* (see page 67) and *Sweet Shop* (see page 57) draw on the traditional genre of the fairytale to structure their modern short stories. Write your introduction to the stories and the fairytale genre. Then use some of the sentence starters below to write your essay. Remember to use quotations from the text to support your points.

- The setting of each story is very distinctive . . .
- The portrayal of the characters in these stories differs from the stereotypes of a traditional fairytale . . .
- The issues examined in each story differ from a traditional fairytale . . .

- Each story is based on a well-known fairytale, and the writer gives us hints and clues that this is the case throughout the story . . .

- The endings of each story are very different from a traditional fairytale . . .

- The story I prefer is . . .
  My reasons are . . .

Chart relating Activities to Framework Objectives for KS3

Title of Story	Main Framework Objectives covered in the Activities:				
	Sentence Level (S)	Text Level – Reading (TR)	Text Level – Writing (TW)	Speaking & Listening (S&L)	Word Level (W)
The Sweeper		7TR12 7TR14	7TW6 7TW12		7W11 7W15
		8TR14	8TW6 8TW12		8W6c 8W11
			9TW5 9TW6		9W5 9W7
The Boys' Toilets			7TW10		
	8S12		8TW12		
	9S3		9TW7		
Sweet Shop		7TR6 7TR7	7TW19		
		8TR5 8TR10 8TR11 8TR14	8TW13 8TW18		
			9TW17		

Title of Story	Sentence Level (S)	Text Level – Reading (TR)	Text Level – Writing (TW)	Speaking & Listening (S&L)	Word Level (W)
The Werewolf	7S1 7S2	7TR8 7TR12	7TW7		7W15
	8S13	8TR14	8TW6 8TW7 8TW8		8W6c 8W7c 8W8 8W11
	9S11	9TR10	9TW5		9W5 9W7
The Adventure of the Sussex Vampire		7TR1 7TR2 7TR6 7TR7 7TR8 7TR12	7TW10 7TW11 7TW19		
		8TR1 8TR2 8TR4 8TR5 8TR10	8TW10 8TW11 8TW18		8W11
		9TR2 9TR4	9TW9 9TW12		9W7

Title of Story	Sentence Level (S)	Text Level – Reading (TR)	Text Level – Writing (TW)	Speaking & Listening (S&L)	Word Level (W)
Lamb to the Slaughter	7S1 7S2	7TR6 7TR7 7TR8 7TR12	7TW7 7TW8 7TW19		
		8TR4 8TR5 8TR7 8TR10 8TR14	8TW6 8TW7 8TW18		8W7c 8W8
			9TW5		9W7
The Knight's Tale	7S18	7TR8 7TR9 7TR12 7TR15 7TR16 7TR20			
	8S13	8TR7 8TR14 8TR15 8TR16			8W11
	9S11	9TR6 9TR15 9TR16			9W7

Title of Story	Sentence Level (S)	Text Level – Reading (TR)	Text Level – Writing (TW)	Speaking & Listening (S&L)	Word Level (W)
Cinderella Girl	7S13b	7TR2 7TR6 7TR8 7TR12	7TW8 7TW10		7W15
	8S9 8S12	8TR4 8TR5	8TW12 8TW13		8W6 8W6c 8W9 8W11
			9TW8 9TW11 9TW13		9W5 9W7
Gift		7TR1 7TR2 7TR8 7TR12 7TR14		7S&L10 7S&L11 7S&L12	
		8TR1 8TR2 8TR4 8TR7 8TR14		8S&L10 8S&L11 8S&L12	8W11
		9TR1 9TR2		9S&L9 9S&L10	9W7

▲

Title of Story	Sentence Level (S)	Text Level – Reading (TR)	Text Level – Writing (TW)	Speaking & Listening (S&L)	Word Level (W)
A Sound of Thunder	7S13e	7TR6 7TR7 7TR8 7TR14	7TW10 7TW15		
	8S8 8S9	8TR4 8TR5 8TR10 8TR14 8TR18	8TW13 8TW14		8W11
			9TW13 9TW17		
Mind Bend		7TR8 7TR14			7W15
		8TR4 8TR14			8W6c 8W11
					9W5

Title of Story	Sentence Level (S)	Text Level – Reading (TR)	Text Level – Writing (TW)	Speaking & Listening (S&L)	Word Level (W)
The Tomb of Sarah	7S1 7S2	7TR8	7TW10 7TW13		7W15
		8TR4 8TR7	8TW10 8TW11		8W6c 8W7c 8W8
			9TW10 9TW12		9W5 9W7
Interview with the Vampire	7S13	7TR8 7TR12	7TW10 7TW13		
	8S9	8TR7 8TR14	8TW10 8TW11		8W11
	9S7 9S8		9TW10 9TW12		9W7

ALSO IN

Heinemann
New Windmills

Founding Editors: Anne and Ian Serraillier

Chinua Achebe Things Fall Apart
David Almond Skellig
Maya Angelou I Know Why the Caged Bird Sings
Margaret Atwood The Handmaid's Tale
Jane Austen Pride and Prejudice
Stan Barstow Joby; A Kind of Loving
Nina Bawden Carrie's War; Kept in the Dark; The Finding; Humbug
Malorie Blackman Tell Me No Lies; Words Last Forever
Ray Bradbury The Golden Apples of the Sun
Melvin Burgess and Lee Hall Billy Elliot
Betsy Byars The Midnight Fox; The Pinballs; The Eighteenth Emergency
Victor Canning The Runaways
Susan Cooper King of Shadows
Robert Cormier We All Fall Down; Heroes
Roald Dahl Danny, The Champion of the World; The Wonderful
Story of Henry Sugar; George's Marvellous Medicine; The Witches;
Boy; Going Solo; Matilda; My Year
Anita Desai The Village by the Sea
Charles Dickens A Christmas Carol; Great Expectations; A Charles
Dickens Selection
Berlie Doherty Granny was a Buffer Girl; Street Child
Roddy Doyle Paddy Clarke Ha Ha Ha
Anne Fine The Granny Project
Jamila Gavin The Wheel of Surya
Graham Greene Brighton Rock
Ann Halam Dr Franklin's Island
Thomas Hardy The Withered Arm and Other Wessex Tales
L P Hartley The Go-Between
Ernest Hemmingway The Old Man and the Sea; A Farewell to Arms
Barry Hines A Kestrel For A Knave
Nigel Hinton Getting Free; Buddy; Buddy's Song; Out of the Darkness
Anne Holm I Am David
Janni Howker Badger on the Barge; The Nature of the Beast;
Martin Farrell

How many have you read?